DEMI-DEVILS

Other books by Charles Norton Coe:

Wordsworth and the Literature of Travel
Shakespeare's Villains

DEMI-DEVILS

The Character of
Shakespeare's Villains

By CHARLES NORTON COE

Professor of English

and

Dean of the Graduate School
Northern Illinois University

BOOKMAN ASSOCIATES, INC.

NEW YORK 3

TO TIM AND DODIE

PREFACE

Since my monograph, *Shakespeare's Villains,* first appeared five years ago, I have read new books and articles on this subject with more than the usual interest. I have also consulted works published prior to 1957 that were not included in my original bibliography. Although this reading has made me look upon my own contribution with increased humility, I still believe there is a place for a basic treatment of Shakespeare's villains. For this reason I have attempted to improve upon my first essay. Like its predecessor, this book is directed at the general student of Shakespeare's plays: the college undergraduate and those whose exposure to Shakespeare comes not in the classroom, but through seeing the plays on the stage or on television. To those specialists whose writing is aimed primarily at other Shakespearean scholars it may seem difficult to justify so elementary a treatment as this. But even though many scholars who might be critical of works such as mine have themselves been teachers of college freshman and sophomore English courses, they seem to forget the state of learning in America. Some of them have objected to my point of departure, namely, the impression Shakespeare's villains would make on an audience viewing a play for the first time. From the point of view of a specialist's knowledge of Shakespeare it may seem incredible that anyone, not still in his early teens, could approach Shakespeare unconditioned by his school training or by what the critics had led (or misled) him to believe. But let us look at the facts. How often does an American student graduate from high school with more than a nodding acquaintance with two or three Shakespearean plays? For the thirty or forty per cent of our high school graduates who go on to college the situation is probably not much better. Excluding majors in English and dramatics, the average college student may be exposed to two or three Shakespearean plays in freshman composition or sophomore literature; more than likely these

7

will be the same plays studied in high school. In short, Shakespeare's audiences—at least in America—approach his plays not with any solid background of Shakespearean criticism, but in blissful ignorance. But if Shakespeare is being studied in school and college proportionately less and less, his plays are being seen more and more in summer theatres, on television, and at the movies, by audiences that know little about him.

In this revision I have treated the same villains as before. My introduction and conclusion, though modified somewhat, remain essentially the same. But the treatment of individual villains in Chapters II-V is more detailed than in the original study.

For permission to quote from copyrighted material I am grateful to the following publishers: American Psychological Association for Irving Edgar, "Shakespeare's Psychopathological Knowledge . . . ," *Journal of Abnormal and Social Psychology,* XXX, I, April-June, 1935, pp. 70-83; Cambridge University Press for M. C. Bradbrook, *Themes and Conventions of Elizabethan Tragedy,* 1935; W. M. T. Dodds, "The Character of Angelo in *Measure for Measure, MLR,* XLI, July, 1946, pp. 246-255; and E. E. Stoll, *Art and Artifice in Shakespeare,* 1938; Columbia University Press for Bernard Spivack, *Shakespeare and the Allegory of Evil,* 1958; Thomas Y. Crowell Company for Bernard Grebanier, *The Heart of Hamlet,* 1960; Ginn and Company for *The Complete Works of Shakespeare,* ed. G. L. Kittredge, 1936, and *The Tragedy of King Lear,* ed. G. L. Kittredge, 1940; Harvard University Press for T. M. Raysor, *Coleridge's Shakespearean Criticism,* 2 vols., 1930; Hillary House, Ltd., for Kenneth Muir, *Shakespeare's Sources I, Comedies and Tragedies,* 1957; Longmans, Green and Company for J. I. M. Stewart, *Character and Motive in Shakespeare,* 1949; Macmillan and Company, Ltd., and St. Martin's Press, Inc., for A. C. Bradley, *Shakespearean Tragedy,* 1926; and J. Palmer, *Comic Characters of Shakespeare,* 1946; Oxford University Press for E. K. Chambers, *William Shakespeare,* 2 vols., 1930; G. W. Knight, *The Shakespearian Tempest,* 1932, and D. N. Smith, *Shakespeare Criticism,* 1916; University of Kentucky Press for Robert Heilman, *Magic in the Web,* 1956; University of North Carolina Press for R. W. Babcock, *The Genesis of Shakespeare Idolatry, 1766-1799,* 1931 and

Ralph M. Sargent, "The Source of *Titus Andronicus, SP,* XLVI, 2, April, 1949, pp. 167-183; Frederick Unger Publishing Company for E. E. Stoll's *Shakespeare Studies,* 1942; Washington Square Press for *The Merchant of Venice,* ed. Wright and Freund, 1957; A. P. Watt & Son for Margaret Webster, *Shakespeare Today,* 1957; Yale University Press for *The Tragedy of Titus Andronicus,* ed. A. M. Witherspoon, 1926.

For his kind assistance in reading proof, I am indebted to Mr. James F. Simon of Northern Illinois University.

C.N.C.

DeKalb, Illinois, May, 1962

A student who undertakes to write on Shakespeare today is confronted by many conflicting points of view. On the one hand, he discovers discouraging comments, such as the following excerpt from a recent review of Shakespearean scholarship, suggesting that there is really nothing new to be said: "The original articles incline to be commonplace or trivial, but there is little left to say about Shakespeare that does not fall into one of these two classifications." [1] On the other hand, he comes across some books on Shakespeare which imply that no one who wrote before the beginning of the present century really understood the bard. For example, an essay published in 1933 informs us that "the assumption that Shakespeare was pre-eminently a great 'creator of characters' " [2] is an irrelevant presupposition. Thus with a flourish some critics seem to dismiss the opinions of Johnson, Coleridge, Hazlitt, Lamb, Bradley, and dozens of others.

What this type of modern scholar is trying to say, I suspect, is that the opinions of earlier writers, so long accepted as gospel, do not seem valid to him. He thinks they are wrong and he is right; but the truth may be that critical opinions fluctuate just as capriciously as do tastes in creative literature. Or perhaps any attempt to assert "the truth" about Shakespeare is presumptuous, as T. S. Eliot apparently thought when he wrote: "About any one so great as Shakespeare it is probable that we can never be right; and if we can never be right, it is better that we should from time to time change our way of being wrong." [3]

In approaching the subject of Shakespeare's villains, I am assuming that the plays were written not primarily to be read and studied but to be acted before an audience. I am aware that this is only one way of looking at the plays and that they do and should yield themselves to other kinds of interpretation. For example, they have provided a fertile field for lovers of poetry and for textual critics; and they are a happy hunting ground for image and symbol seekers and for those scholars who delight in counting the number of times an author uses words like *noble, moon,* or *bloody.*

I believe that whatever approach one makes to Shakespeare, there is much that can be learned, and that some contribution, however slight, may be made; for, "It is the duty of every professor of literature to say his say on Shakespeare and on what Shakespeare means to the world. To shrink from the task is immoral: to face it, is . . . to expose one's own unworthiness." [4]

I am indebted to Mrs. Charles F. Hudson and Professor Theodore A. Sherman, both of the University of Idaho, for their kind assistance in reading proof.

Finally, I wish to acknowledge my gratitude to the Regents and Administration of the University of Idaho for granting me a leave of absence to complete the research for this book.

C.N.C.

New Haven, Connecticut, August, 1956

TABLE OF CONTENTS

I. INTRODUCTION

Dr. Johnson once remarked that some people "seem to admire indiscriminately whatever has been long preserved."[1] A student need not search far in literary criticism to uncover evidence supporting this statement. For example, Shakespeare has been praised for almost every artistic and literary quality imaginable. In many cases the praise has been just or even inadequate; yet sometimes uncritical recognition of his genius has led to praise of qualities which he did not possess. Prior to the twentieth century it was generally assumed that, in the realistic and psychologically accurate portrayal of character, Shakespeare left little to be desired. In fact, it was probably because Shakespeare's characters attracted such favorable attention by at least as early as the eighteenth century that adverse criticism began to give way to more sympathetic attitudes. Tracing the phases of eighteenth century criticism in *The Genesis of Shakespeare Idolatry,* Robert W. Babcock writes:

> During the earlier period, from 1660 to 1730, the traditional objections to Shakespeare generally held sway . . . the critics castigated the poet for neglecting the unities, for ignoring the ancients, for violating decorum by resorting to tragicomedy and supernatural characters, and for using puns and blank verse. But after 1730 . . . Shakespeare's characters were wholesomely applauded, the poet was promoted to the rank of conscious artist, and he was studied sympathetically with reference to his own age.[2]

Though Johnson, like Pope, wrote with reservation about Shakespeare's ability as a poet, they agreed in praising his powers of characterization. The former writes:

> [Shakespeare's] characters are so copiously diversified, and some of them so justly pursued, that his works may be considered as a map of life, a faithful miniature of human

15

transactions, and he that has read Shakespeare with attention will perhaps find little new in the crowded world.[3]

And in the preface to his edition of Shakespeare, Pope tells us
that "every single character in *Shakespear* is as much an Individual, as those in Life itself." [4] Extravagant as these claims may
seem, there was at least some restraint in the comments of Pope
and Johnson. In fact, D. Nichol Smith, in his *Shakespeare Criticism,* calls Johnson:

> the last great representative of what may be called the judi-
> cial manner. He is the true successor of Dryden, who looked
> upon Shakespeare as a brother dramatist, certainly of sur-
> passing genius, but not therefore beyond the pale of censure.
> Johnson never ran any risk of forgetting that Shakespeare
> was an author who had to write for his living.[5]

After Pope and Johnson helped pave the way for praise of Shakespeare's powers of characterization, critics like Maurice Morgann, Lamb, Coleridge, and Hazlitt went a step further. They
were not satisfied to regard Shakespeare as a craftsman of the
stage creating dramatic characters; they preferred to view the
make-believe world of his creation as a world of real men and
women. The *locus classicus* of this viewpoint is found in a foot-
note to Morgann's essay on Falstaff in which he insists that
Shakespeare's characters should be regarded "rather as Historic
than Dramatic beings." [6]

By the nineteenth century bardolatry was in full sway; na-
tionalistic pride and even reverential awe were evident in the
critics' attitude: "The Englishman," writes Coleridge, "who without reverence, a proud and affectionate reverence, can utter the
name of William Shakespeare, stands disqualified for the office of
critic." [7] "It may be said of Shakespear," exclaims Hazlitt in his
Characters of Shakespeare's Plays, "that 'those who are not for
him are against him' . . . An overstrained enthusiasm is more
pardonable with respect to Shakespear than the want of it." [8]
Just how strained this enthusiasm could become may be seen by
reading Swinburne's eloquent tribute:

> The word Shakespeare connotes more than any other man's
> name that ever was written or spoken upon earth. The

bearer of that name was the one supreme creator of men who ever arose among mortals to show them and to leave with them an all but innumerable race of evident and indisputable immortals. No child of man and woman was too high or too low for his perfect apprehension and appreciation. Of good and evil, in all their subtlest and sublimest forms of thought and action and revelation, he knew more than ever it has been given to any other man to know.[9]

Even when nineteenth century critics *seem* to be qualifying their praise, they usually do so paradoxically, as in Lamb's equivocal remark (reasserted in the present century by Logan P. Smith),[10] that "the plays of Shakspeare are less calculated for performance on a stage, than those of almost any other dramatist whatever." On first reading, this suggests that one of the world's greatest dramatists produced plays unsuitable for stage production. If this really were Lamb's verdict, it would be a surprising one to come from such a lover of the theatre. On examining Lamb's essay more closely, however, one gets a clearer insight into his meaning: calling attention to this *seeming* fault is Lamb's whimsical way of praising the master. Lamb means that the intimate life-like scenes, "the love-dialogues of Romeo and Juliet," "the more intimate and sacred sweetness of nuptial colloquy between an Othello or a Posthumus with their married wives," lose some of their effectiveness "by the inherent fault of stage representation." Nor does Lamb appreciate hearing Hamlet's soliloquies declaimed as they must be if a large audience is to hear these most personal and intimate musings. "I am not arguing that Hamlet should not be acted, but how much Hamlet is made another thing by being acted." In Lamb's strictures, especially his statement that "the Lear of Shakspeare cannot be acted," [11] we note a salient quality of nineteenth century criticism: it was personal and lacking in objectivity; it was written by men some of whom were themselves great creative writers. But they tended to distort Shakespeare by subordinating interest in the plays as drama to their almost exclusive concern for interpreting characters .

In view of this indiscriminate praise of Shakespeare, especially for his fidelity to human nature, it was inevitable that a reaction would set in. Some critics of the present century, suspicious of Romantic enthusiasm and inclined toward skepticism and iconoclasm, chose as one of their targets, not Shakespeare himself, but what his earlier critics had made of him. Though some of Professor Stoll's arguments were anticipated by Robert Bridges, Tolstoy, and Levin Schücking, Stoll probably represents the most persistent of twentieth century research scholars who have sought to stem the flow of uncritical praise for Shakespeare's characters by applying historical perspective to their criticism. Stoll writes:

> Heaven and earth have been moved to establish the true text, to interpret a now forgotten phrase or track down an obscure allusion; but of the larger meaning, the conception of a character, and the scope and significance of the whole, each man feels (or writes as if he felt) pretty free to think what he pleases.[12]

Stoll makes clear what the starting point of his investigation is to be: "The dramatist's intention—that, I must believe, together with his success or failure in fulfilling it, is the only matter of importance." [13] In attempting to readjust the overemphasis on character, Stoll appeals to Aristotle's dictum that tragedy is an imitation of action, not character. Stoll's implication here is that nineteenth century critics, with their interest in personalities, lost sight of the function of drama as a whole and placed undue emphasis on character. Stoll's argument was anticipated by an expert on the theatre, George Pierce Baker, who, in *The Development of Shakespeare as a Dramatist,* insists that Shakespeare's audience was more interested in story, plot, and action than in character:

> what they [the average audience] are watching and what they are enjoying is not the characterization of Hamlet, of Lear, of Macbeth, or Othello, but the stories in which these men are the central figures . . . the world in general finds its delight . . . not in character, but in story . . . It is, broadly speaking, only the trained and critical part of an audience which thinks more of characterization than story.[14]

Besides attempting to correct the overemphasis on character apparent in earlier criticism and to assert the importance of action in a play, Stoll and others tried to prove that Shakespeare wrote with the demands and interests of Elizabethan audiences foremost in mind. For example, with reference to Shakespeare's powers of characterization, much has recently been said regarding conventions of the theatre.

> It is only during the last dozen years [wrote Muriel C. Bradbrook in 1935] that there has been any attempt to discover the conventions behind Shakespeare's characterization. . . . The plays were read [by nineteenth century critics] as poetic romances rather than as drama, and this meant that the action became altogether subordinated to the character. . . . Coleridge's psychological bent and Lamb's gregariousness turned all the characters into real human beings.[15]

The extent to which twentieth century historical critics have rejected nineteenth century interpretations of Shakespeare's characters may be seen by examining some of the conventions that apply specifically to villains. 1) We are told that, by Elizabethan audiences, villains were accepted with or without motivation. They were accepted as types because they were black like Aaron, deformed like Richard III, Italian like Iago, or illegitimate like Edmund. This convention is offered to explain what, to some modern critics, appears to be insufficient motivation in Shakespeare's villains. Of Iago, Miss Bradbrook writes: "he is plainly a villain, as he is at pains to expound in soliloquy. Villains are villains; there is no need to ask why. . . . Besides, he is an Italian, and therefore . . . treacherous, jealous and Machiavellian." [16] 2) Elizabethan audiences sometimes regarded villains as stock comic characters. Yet nineteenth century critics tended to overlook this convention and extended sympathy to villains like Shylock. Heine, for example, commenting on a performance of *The Merchant of Venice,* describes "a beautiful pale Englishwoman [who] burst into tears at the end of the fourth act, crying out several times, 'the poor man [Shylock] is wronged'." [17] But, however the role of Shylock has been interpreted, some twentieth century critics tell us categorically that, in extending sympathy to a villain like Shylock, we are overlooking a convention of the times which obviously saw in him a stock comic character. 3) Elizabethans regarded evil differently than do modern playgoers. Stoll advances this argument to ac-count for what he regards as our inability to understand how Shakespeare's villains should be interpreted:

> Two notions to-day possess us—that man, though often per-verted, is not evil or in love with evil, and that he is the creature of heredity and environment. Neither idea plays any part, philosophically or practically, in Shakespeare, and yet people freely find it there.[18]

4) Villains explain and boast of their villainy to the audience, and even praise the heroes. This practice, though perhaps not lifelike, is necessary for effective exposition. According to Stew-art, "Schücking's first discovery about Shakespeare's characters is this: that the dramatist frequently makes them speak of them-selves with an unnatural objectivity, in order that the audience may easily understand their roles." [19] 5) There is a convention that disguises will be convincing even though the audience must obviously be able to recognize the character through his disguise. 6) Slander will be believed even though the person slandered is loved and trusted, and the slanderer is of dubious character. 7) Finally, if the incidents seem absurd, as in Lear's dividing his kingdom—an act that leads to all manner of villainy—we are told that the story was so well known by Elizabethan audiences that its incredibility would be overlooked. To cite Bradbrook again,

> there were those old and familiar stories which relied on folk traditions. The kind of realism which these tales have is not dependent on the plausibility of the incidents, but upon the fact that they are woven into the people's very ways of thinking and feeling.[20]

Part of my purpose in analyzing eleven of Shakespeare's vil-lains will be to show how these conventions apply and to what extent an awareness of them should provide reasons for mod-ifying earlier opinions about the lifelike quality of Shakespeare's characters. Before I begin my analysis, I want to point out that the test of a character in a play should be the effect he makes on the audience, not on the scholarly reader. We should not have to be reminded of this except that the critical approach to

Shakespeare usually neglects the viewpoint of the playgoer; and it seems to me unreasonable that adverse criticism of Shakespeare's powers of creating characters should be based on careful readings and rereadings of the plays with a microscopic search for flaws and inconsistencies. I do not believe that drama should be subjected to that type of scrutiny. How common this microscopic approach is, however, can be seen by quoting from G. Wilson Knight's *Shakespearian Tempest:*

> After reading *Macbeth,* we tend to remember the chief persons, and the story: all the rest, the child symbolism, the varied atmospheric suggestion, the tempests and strange screams of death, all this is only appreciated *after years of study.* (Italics mine.) [21]

Certainly many of Shakespeare's plays deserve years of study, and one should be grateful for any new light shed on critical and textual problems. At the same time, I think we are justified in discounting flaws and inconsistencies in characterization that would not be apparent to a spectator seeing the play. What Mary Lascelles wrote in her study of *Measure for Measure* could apply as a test to other plays. "The dominant question to be considered is this: does the whole, or a substantial part . . . of the play make *stage sense?* Does it yield a practicable and . . . intelligible stage performance?" [22]

It is also necessary, before discussing the question of whether specific characters are lifelike, to define "lifelike" by setting up certain criteria as a base for judgment; for though I do not wish to discount the conventions listed earlier, I think it can be shown that some psychological accuracy is required for effective characterization. First, the characters should appear to have reasons of their own for their behavior. This is important because plays are written so that the characters and the plot supplement each other; and if it appears to the audience that a character acts only to further the interests of plot, we say that the character is not realistic. The crudest of Elizabethan villains, according to Bradbrook, "are hardly ever interesting. Their business was to complicate the action and produce the tragic situation." [23] One purpose of realistic characterization is to lend credibility to what is not real; one way that this can be done is to make it appear that villains have wills of their own and act with their own interests, rather than those of the plot, in mind. This motivation is obviously a most important element in characterization. We should expect a villain without adequate motivation to be unconvincing and therefore unsatisfactory. In evaluating the characterization of Shakespeare's villains it will be interesting to note in which plays Shakespeare improved the motivation he found in his prototypes, and in which plays the motivation is not as convincing as that in the sources.

There is another essential item in realistic characterization: variety or complexity in character presentation. This many-sidedness may consist of qualities closely related to the plot, such as remorse or hypocrisy in a villain; or it may bear little relation to the action of the play and serve merely to round out the character. A character in a play will seem more realistic when several sides of his personality are revealed; whereas a character who only loves or who only fights, and who is never represented as doing anything else, may seem less convincing.

Bearing in mind these criteria which should aid us in determining whether or not a character is realistically portrayed, and remembering also the stage conventions discussed earlier, let us examine several of Shakespeare's villains. How shall we organize our discussion? Does an examination of the dates on which the plays were composed reveal any tendency toward greater psychological accuracy of character portrayal as Shakespeare gained experience in writing? Excluding for the moment Claudius and the three chief villains in *Lear,* let us consider the following grouping. I have placed the villains in two columns with Kittredge's dates of composition in parentheses:

Aaron	(1592)	Iago	(1604)
Angelo	(1604)	Shylock	(1596)
Richard III	(1592)	Macbeth	(1606)

In this limited sampling chronology is suggestive, but not conclusive. Though no critic would deny progress in lifelike characterization in the twelve year span between Aaron and Iago, and though most critics would see significant development in the fourteen years between Richard III and Macbeth, few would

suggest that Angelo is more effectively characterized than Shylock even though *The Merchant of Venice* was written eight
years earlier than *Measure for Measure.* Looking at the columns
vertically, we note that Aaron, who will turn out to be the least
convincing villain we are to examine, appears in a play written
in the same year as *Richard III.*

I raise the question of the development of Shakespeare's
powers in characterizing villains because some critics, with a
loyalty to Shakespeare that is touching though not particularly
discerning, have accused me of ignoring chronology in evaluating
Shakespeare's treatment of characters: "Professor Coe seems to
allow no theory of Shakespeare's developing technique: Aaron
is compared unfavorably with Iago as if it were Shakespeare's
fault." [24] Actually I have no reluctance to allow a theory of
Shakespeare's developing technique—in fact, I would assume
one—but the evidence of chronology is inconclusive with reference to the villains we are about to discuss.

Turning then from a consideration based on the date of
composition of the plays in which these characters appear, but
using the same two columns of villains, is there any other basis
by which Aaron can profitably be compared with Iago, Angelo
with Shylock, and Richard III with Macbeth? Yes, because Aaron
and Iago are commonly classified as Machiavels; Angelo and
Shylock are both characters whose villainy is thwarted in comedies; and Richard III and Macbeth have in common achieving
and maintaining kingdoms through murder. Though other factors besides the characterization of these villains contribute to
the relative success or failure of their plays, an examination of
Shakespeare's technique in character-drawing may help, both in
defining more precisely what constitutes lifelike characterization
and in determining what bearing characterization has on the
total effect of his plays.

In addition to the three pairs of villains listed above, I shall
discuss Edmund, Regan, Goneril, and Claudius. I group these
last four villains separately because they do not dominate their
plays to the same extent that the first six villains do. Both of the
tragedies in which these villains appear belong to the period of
Shakespeare's maturity—*Hamlet,* 1600-1601; *Lear,* 1605-1606; but

whatever generalizations can be made about the development of Shakespeare as a dramatist, the chronological evidence will again be inconclusive here unless one is willing to conclude that Edmund, Regan, and Goneril are more effectively characterized than Richard III, Shylock, Claudius, and Iago.

II. AARON AND IAGO

A comparison between Aaron and Iago should provide a suitable beginning for our discussion of Shakespeare's villains. In these two characters we shall probably find the worst and best examples of Shakespeare's skill in characterization. An examination of Aaron should support my contention that the typical, indiscriminate praise of Shakespeare for creating characters who are invariably true to life will not stand the test of careful investigation. An analysis of Iago will show that the opposite viewpoint, namely, that Shakespeare was not concerned with drawing real characters with convincing motivation and lifelike personalities, but that he was merely using stock characters and relying on well-established stage conventions, is equally erroneous when applied to his most successful creations.

In the history of literary criticism there have been many vicissitudes, both in Shakespeare's general reputation and in the relative popularity of his plays. Nowhere is this latter fluctuation more remarkable than in the stage history of *Titus Andronicus.* According to Professor Witherspoon, "During the first three decades of its existence, *Titus* was one of the most popular of all the plays attributed to Shakespeare; for the last three hundred years it has had almost the scantiest stage history of them all." [1] Critics who write so enthusiastically about Shakespeare's powers of characterization seem to have forgotten the almost inhuman cruelty of Aaron, villain in this earliest Shakespearean tragedy of blood and horror. Indeed, it may have been the unwillingness of early scholars to accept *Titus Andronicus* as Shakespeare's own work that gave impetus to the controversy over the authorship of the play even though it was included in the First Folio of 1623 brought out by Heminge and Condell, friends and fellow-actors of Shakespeare, and was mentioned as follows by Francis Meres in his *Palladis Tamia,* 1598: "As Plautus and Seneca are accounted the best for comedy and tragedy among the Latins, so Shakespeare among the English is the most excellent in both kinds . . . witness his . . . *Richard III, Henry IV, King John, Titus Andronicus,* and his *Romeo and Juliet.*" [2] Kittredge's explanation regarding the origin of the dispute over the authorship of *Titus Andronicus,* and his conclusion that the play is Shakespeare's, follows:

> Shakespeare's connection with TITUS ANDRONICUS has been a moot question for two centuries and a half, ever since the irresponsible minor playwright Edward Ravenscroft . . . acknowledged his indebtedness to [*Titus*] and remarked, 'I have been told by some anciently conversant with the Stage, that it was not Originally [Shakespeare's,] but brought by a private Authour to be Acted, and he only gave some Master-touches to one or two of the . . . Characters.' The idle gossip which he reports (or invents) cannot weigh against the positive assertion of Meres—made in 1598, when the play was only five or six years old—that it is one of Shakespeare's 'excellent' tragedies. Nobody would have listened to Ravenscroft but for the feeling that TITUS ANDRONICUS is too horrible to be Shakespeare's. But Shakespeare was always prone to try experiments, and it would be strange if he had not written one out-and-out tragedy of blood when Kyd had shown how powerfully such things appealed to playgoers.[3]

Although that controversy is about all that keeps the play alive today, it cannot detain us here. Our concern is with Aaron, earliest of Shakespeare's Machiavellians and prototype of the more successful but not entirely convincing Richard III, as well as of Iago, generally acknowledged to be one of the great Shakespearean villains. But *Titus Andronicus,* which was written about 1592, is a far cry from either *Richard III* or *Othello.* After its initial popularity it has scarcely been acted at all. Its failure may be due, in part, to the unrealistic characterization of Aaron, who seems almost inhuman in his cruelty. Aaron's motivation could have been made convincing because he is first introduced to the audience as a prisoner of the Romans; and, like Tamora, Chiron, and Demetrius, Aaron witnesses the cruel treatment accorded to Alarbus, Tamora's eldest son and one of the prisoners. Lucius asks his father, Titus Andronicus, for

> the proudest prisoner of the Goths,
> That we may hew his limbs and on a pile
> *Ad manes fratrum* sacrifice his flesh.   (I:i:96-98) [4]

In spite of Tamora's plea for mercy, the execution, which Titus explains as a religious sacrifice to avenge the memory of his own sons who have been slain in battle—"T'appease their groaning shadows that are gone" (I:i:126)—is accomplished; and Lucius reports to his father and to the surviving prisoners:

> See, lord and father, how we have perform'd
> Our Roman rites. Alarbus' limbs are lopp'd
> And entrails feed the sacrificing fires,
> Whose smoke like incense doth perfume the sky.
> (I:i:142-145)

Thus the initial atrocity in this bloody play can be charged to the Roman general, Titus Andronicus, and to his son, Lucius. Tamora, who seems at first to be the chief villain in the play— Aaron appears but does not speak during the first act—has a comprehensible motive for her revenge; and her remark, "I'll find a day to massacre them all" (I:i:450), is understandable to the audience, even though some of her subsequent conduct may not be. But, although Tamora (like Lady Macbeth) takes the initiative and plots revenge against the Romans, she soon relinquishes the main role to Aaron who is rightly described as the "Chief architect and plotter of these woes" (V:iii:122).

Since Aaron was captured by the Romans and since Tamora is in love with him, his sympathy for and assistance in her plan for revenge might have been made understandable. What makes Aaron seem like the personification of evil instead of a convincing character is his protestation, on several occasions, of delight in villainy. His first soliloquy at the beginning of act two is necessary for expository purposes; his first conversation with Tamora is also part of the exposition, essential if the audience is to know who will be Tamora's chief ally in revenge. In tactfully turning down Tamora's suggestion that they enjoy the seclusion of a lonely part of the forest for love-making, Aaron shows that his mood is not amorous, but vengeful:

No, madam, these are no Venereal signs.
Vengeance is in my heart, death in my hand,
Blood and revenge are hammering in my head.
Hark, Tamora, the empress of my soul,
Which never hopes more heaven than rests in thee—
This is the day of doom for Bassianus;
His Philomel must lose her tongue to-day,
Thy sons make pillage of her chastity
And wash their hands in Bassianus' blood.   (II:iii:37-45)

So far, Aaron's motivation is reasonably convincing, especially
since he seems to be assuming the role of accomplice to his lover,
Tamora. The audience might even sympathize with Tamora and
Aaron, especially since Titus Andronicus, nominally the hero
of the play, is introduced in so unfavorable a light. Besides his
deafness to Tamora's plea already referred to, Titus kills one of
his own sons, Mutius, who helps Bassianus take Lavinia from
Saturninus. We shall note a similar, though not so serious, a flaw
in characterization later in this study when we consider the early
behavior of King Lear.

But what makes Aaron's behavior unconvincing as the play
develops is his fiendish delight in villainy. He is like Iago in the
relish with which he plots and observes the destruction of his
enemies without having Iago's motivation or some of Iago's re-
deeming features—features, it is hardly necessary to add, that
redeem Iago, not morally, but as a plausible character in a play.

Let us observe some of Aaron's villainy. He incites Demetrius
and Chiron to rape and mutilate Lavinia; he pins the blame
for Bassianus' murder on Martius and Quintus; he tricks Titus
into believing that the emperor will pardon his two sons if Titus
will send the emperor his own hand. Aaron's reaction to this last
fiendish trick is representative of his attitude toward villainy in
general. Titus lets Aaron cut off his hand, believing that it will
buy the falsely promised pardon.

AARON: I go, Andronicus; and for thy hand
Look by-and-by to have thy sons with thee.
[Aside] Their heads, I mean. O, how this villainy
Doth fat me with the very thoughts of it!

Let fools do good, and fair men call for grace,
Aaron will have his soul black like his face.   (III:i:201-206)

The only time Aaron acts with his own personal interest in mind is on the occasion when he saves his infant son from Demetrius who threatens to "broach the tadpole on my rapier's point" (IV:ii:85). At this threat the parental instinct is aroused, and Aaron shouts:

Sooner this sword shall plough thy bowels up. . . .
Stay, murtherous villains! Will you kill your brother?
Now by the burning tapers of the sky,
That shone so brightly when this boy was got,
He dies upon my scimitar's sharp point
That touches this my first-born son and heir. . . .
This before all the world do I prefer;
This maugre all the world will I keep safe,
Or some of you shall smoke for it in Rome!   (IV:ii:87-111)

Aaron's behavior in this scene is more personally motivated than his other actions. Even his murdering the nurse who brings him his baby is motivated by a wish to protect the child rather than by his delight in villainy. To prevent the outcry that might result from discovering that the empress had given birth to a black boy, Aaron also arranges to have a new-born white baby substituted for his own. In attempting to escape to the Goths with his child, he is captured and brought before the exiled Lucius who recognizes him as "the incarnate devil/That robb'd Andronicus of his good hand" (V:i:40-41). Lucius proposes to hang the child in Aaron's presence; to save the baby, Aaron offers to reveal to Lucius the full extent of his villainy. In confessing, Aaron acts to save his child's life; except for this act of generosity, however, he is the same old Aaron, delighting in the recollection of villainy just as he had earlier relished planning his heinous deeds. Aaron's confession starts with his statement that he begot the black child "on the Empress" (V:i:87). He next admits having advised Tamora's two sons, Demetrius and Chiron, to murder Bassianus and to rape and disfigure Lavinia. He also acknowledges that he implicated Martius and Quintus in the murder of Bassianus. In recounting all this to Lucius, Aaron is

not contrite; on the contrary, he describes his reactions as follows:

> I play'd the cheater for thy father's hand,
> And when I had it, drew myself apart
> And almost broke my heart with extreme laughter.
> I pried me through the crevice of a wall
> When for his hand he had his two sons' heads,
> Beheld his tears, and laugh'd so heartily
> That both mine eyes were rainy like to his.   (V:i:111-117)

Aaron becomes for us no product of that "one supreme creator"
whom Swinburne extols; he is merely an agent to further the
action. We are given few clues as to his background. He is bad
because the plot requires a villain.

> LUCIUS: Art thou not sorry for these heinous deeds?
> AARON: Ay, that I had not done a thousand more.
> Even now I curse the day (and yet I think
> Few come within the compass of my curse)
> Wherein I did not some notorious ill:
> As kill a man, or else devise his death;
> Ravish a maid, or plot the way to do it;
> Accuse some innocent, and forswear myself;
> Set deadly enmity between two friends;
> Make poor men's cattle break their necks;
> Set fire on barns and hay-stacks in the night
> And bid the owners quench them with their tears.
> Oft have I digg'd up dead men from their graves
> And set them upright at their dear friends' door
> Even when their sorrow almost was forgot,
> And on their skins, as on the bark of trees,
> Have with my knife carved in Roman letters
> 'Let not your sorrow die, though I am dead.'
> Tut, I have done a thousand dreadful things
> As willingly as one would kill a fly;
> And nothing grieves me heartily indeed
> But that I cannot do ten thousand more.   (V:i:123-144)

> AARON. Ah, why should wrath be mute and fury dumb?
> I am no baby, I, that with base prayers

I should repent the evils I have done.
Ten thousand worse than ever yet I did
Would I perform if I might have my will.
If one good deed in all my life I did,
I do repent it from my very soul.   (V:iii:184-190)

As these passages show, Aaron is little more than a type, and
Elizabethan audiences would recognize him as such; for, according to Elizabethan psychology, Aaron's blackness alone would
do much to account for his villainy, since audiences in Shakespeare's day believed that there was a "close correspondence between outer seeming and inner being," [5] and that physical beauty
tended to signify goodness, whereas ugliness was associated with
evil.

Another serious defect in Aaron's characterization is his lack
of variety and complexity. It will be illuminating to compare
him with villains like Iago and Richard III who appear more
lifelike because, though villainous, they are characterized as
witty, humorous, and lively, as we shall see when considering
them. Consequently they possess a verisimilitude that is almost
totally lacking in the colorless Aaron. Aaron is unvariable; one
can almost always predict what he is going to do.

Shakespeare wrote *Titus Andronicus* in 1592 when *The Spanish Tragedy,* which appeared about three years earlier, was still
regarded as the most popular Elizabethan tragedy; and, in imi-
tating it, as G. B. Harrison says in *Shakespeare's Tragedies,*
Shakespeare prepared a plot "compared with [which] the *Spanish Tragedy* is milk diet." Elizabethan audiences "gaped at the
horrors of the *Spanish Tragedy;* [Shakespeare] would dislocate
their jaws." [6] In such a play action is paramount; characterization does not assume the importance that is to distinguish much
of Shakespeare's later writing. Even so, Shakespeare does make
use of the Machiavellian Aaron, a character type he developed
more fully in Richard III and Iago. According to Ralph M.
Sargent, Shakespeare's source may have been *The History of
Titus Andronicus.*

In the prose history, the Moor never emerges as an independent character; he remains, until his concluding confession, the instrument of the Queen. The prose history con-

centrates its whole story on the conflict between the two antagonists, Andronicus and the Queen. But Shakespeare's Moor, Aaron, takes on an independent existence and ambition and initiative of his own." [7]

Though Professor Sargent regards this development of Aaron as giving the Moor an element of individuality, actually the prominence of Aaron, whose motivation is less convincing than that of Tamora, merely adds more villainy to a play that has little else. A concentration of the conflict between two principal antagonists might have made better theatre. And as we shall see later in this book, even where the conflict between good and evil is more clearly shown—as in *Lear*—too much villainy of the type in which Edmund, Goneril, and Regan indulge, baffles the understanding and seems incredible on the stage.

By way of summary, the most that can be said of Aaron is that he is a readily accepted and conventional type. He is given little motivation or individuality; he is certainly no outstanding product of that artistic touch with which Shakespeare was presumably endowed and which, according to Pope, never failed him when it came to creating lifelike characters. Of course, one should not be surprised at Shakespeare's shallow characterization of Aaron at this early stage of his dramatic career; for, in using such a villain, Shakespeare undoubtedly realized that he was availing himself of a character with whom the theatre-going public was already well acquainted, the familiar Machiavel. Consequently, his audience would expect less in the way of detailed characterization. An awareness of Aaron's flatness tends, however, to modify the claims of those whom I have called the indiscriminating critics, those who tend to be all-inclusive rather than selective when they praise Shakespeare's characters.

It was once fashionable among scholars to deal with any play or passage of Shakespeare's that did not measure up to his very best by writing it off as the work of another author. Although this practice is no longer common, some critics still seem to resent any suggestion that Shakespeare should be held accountable for his inferior work. They prefer to explain whatever falls short of his best in terms of the conventions of the age or changing styles in dramatic production. For example, in my monograph I was criticized as follows: "Where this book suffers is in its disregard of the difference in dramatic style between the tragic writings of the early 1590's *(Titus, Richard III)* and the more 'realistic' Jacobean tragedy: Coe is simply inclined to blame the one for not being the other." [8] Of course, anyone who has studied the development of British drama is aware of these differences; but what I am concerned with here is the contribution that lifelike characterization can make toward the universal and timeless appeal of Shakespeare's best plays.

The fate of *Titus Andronicus* on the boards should also be considered in evaluating the arguments offered by critics who appeal to the conventions of the Elizabethan stage. If we were to believe them, Aaron's lack of plausible motivation would not have detracted from his effectiveness. "Villains are villains; there is no need to ask why." But some people will ask why, and their questions may have had some effect on the early decline in popularity of *Titus Andronicus*.

Even critics who are skeptical about the verisimilitude of Shakespeare's characters praise the characterization of Iago, though not without some reservation. According to Professor Stoll: "Of Elizabethan Machiavels and villains the greatest is Iago, the culmination of the development through Aaron and Richard III." [9] And speaking of the play as a whole, Bradbrook writes: "*Othello* is perhaps the most brilliantly constructed of all Elizabethan plays. Here, if anywhere, slander is made credible, and the movement of the hero's mind from security through doubt to a conviction by slander is adequately shown." [10]

The reason for this praise can be seen by comparing Iago with Aaron and with Richard III, whom we shall consider next. In Iago there is both motivation and liveliness, qualities we found lacking in Aaron; there is also less implausibility of detail than we shall discover in *Richard III*. Of the motives Shakespeare gives Iago, the first is a plausible one and would probably satisfy the average person seeing the play. The opening scene, with its explanation of Iago's feeling toward Othello and Cassio, sounds convincing:

RODERIGO: Thou told'st me thou didst hold him [Othello]
in thy hate.
IAGO: Despise me if I do not. Three great ones of the city,
In personal suit to make me his lieutenant,
Off-capp'd to him; and, by the faith of man,
I know my price, I am worth no worse a place.
But he, as loving his own pride and purposes,
Evades them with a bombast circumstance,
Horribly stuff'd with epithets of war;
And, in conclusion,
Nonsuits my mediators; for, 'Certes,' says he,
'I have already chose my officer.'
And what was he?
Forsooth, a great arithmetician,
One Michael Cassio, a Florentine
(A fellow almost damn'd in a fair wife),
That never set a squadron in the field,
Nor the division of a battle knows
More than a spinster; unless the bookish theoric,
Wherein the toged consuls can propose
As masterly as he. Mere prattle, without practice,
Is all his soldiership. But he, sir, had th'election;
And I (of whom his eyes had seen the proof
At Rhodes, at Cyprus, and on other grounds
Christian and heathen) must be belee'd and calm'd
By debitor and creditor, this counter-caster.
He (in good time!) must his lieutenant be,
And I (God bless the mark!) his Moorship's ancient.
                                    (I:i:7-33)

Admitting that Iago is underestimating Cassio's ability, it is
not difficult to sympathize with a person who sees one of his
juniors receive the promotion that he himself had expected.
Bradley points out that there is no evidence that Cassio was
Iago's junior either in years or in length of service and warns
students of the play against believing anything Iago says.[11] But
when we consider that the speech just quoted comes at the beginning of the play, I think we must conclude that its purpose
is expository. The audience has not had time to evaluate the
integrity of the characters involved and is chiefly interested in

what is about to happen. Whether Iago's remarks just quoted or his subsequent complaint,

> 'tis the curse of service.
> Preferment goes by letter and affection,
> And not by old gradation, where each second
> Stood heir to th'first   (I:i:35-38),

accurately describes his claims and those of his rival for the lieutenancy, is relatively unimportant at this point in the play. In fact, Iago is inconsistent in evaluating his rival. After having deprecated Cassio's soldierly qualities at the opening of the play, he later tells Montano, "[Cassio] is a soldier fit to stand by Caesar/And give direction" (II:iii:127-128). Still, an audience would be quick to recognize Iago's complaint as the motivating force for his subsequent treachery. It is an only slightly less plausible motive because the statement is unfair to Cassio; certainly most people in the audience, if they stopped to think about it at all, would realize how lacking in objectivity one's views tend to be on the subject of his own merit.

Many critics, however, have questioned Iago's motivation. In a brilliant chapter of his book, *Magic in the Web,* Professor Heilman begins by analyzing Iago's most obvious grounds for enmity against Othello and finds them unconvincing. It is true that, if Othello had been obviously unfair to Iago in giving the lieutenancy to Cassio, Iago's motivation would have been stronger. As Heilman explains, "The question, then, is whether Iago's hope, if it actually did exist, was a reasonable one and whether the disparity between his talents and deserts and those of Cassio was such that Othello's choice was a real injustice to Iago." [12] Heilman then proceeds to list arguments pro and con which, while they are of great interest to the thoughtful student of Shakespeare, are somewhat beside the point if we consider the impression the play makes on the spectator. Some of the facts and opinions to which Heilman calls attention are too involved and detailed for the average theater-goer to observe. For example, Heilman points out that, after I:i:39, "Iago himself never again mentions his loss of the lieutenancy." [13] Possibly Iago's motivation would have seemed more convincing if he had harped on his loss, but his repeated references to his hatred of Othello would probably be understood by an audience to stem from this early grievance; and, even if the grievance is unreasonable, the audience can readily understand Iago's chagrin and enmity, if not the extent to which his desire for revenge leads him. More important, the fact that Iago does not make frequent references to his loss of the lieutenancy is not so significant a *negative* factor in his characterization as is the prominence of his first complaint a *positive* factor.

The most serious flaw in Heilman's argument regarding the implausibility of Iago's motive comes when Heilman summarizes his point of view as follows: "If Iago hurries over the contention that he has been treated unjustly, never recurs to it again, and thus is unconvincing in this matter, what does he say that is convincing?" [14] I do not agree with Heilman's assumption that Iago is unconvincing in this matter. Iago's first speech is given a prominent position at the beginning of the play and occupies thirty-nine lines. I do not call this hurrying over his grievance. Heilman answers his own question, "What does Iago say that is convincing?" by citing five occasions on which Iago verbalizes his hatred of the Moor.[15] Heilman treats these expressions of hatred as though they were somehow disassociated from or even antecedent to Iago's initial grievance at not receiving the lieutenancy. Is it not more reasonable to assume that spectators watching *Othello* would regard Iago's hatred as growing out of his grievance? In a sense, then, Iago's repeatedly asserting his hatred of the Moor is a shorter way of saying that he hates him because Othello did not give him the lieutenancy.

It would be unfair to Heilman's carefully worked out analysis not to concede that the most impressive parts of his theorizing come after the arguments with which I have taken issue. Heilman considers Iago's enmity with all that is good and decent in human relations as part of the villain's depraved nature, and he assumes that this trait antedates the opening of the drama. "Since the malice comes before the occasion that brings it into play, we might say that Iago is 'original evil.' " [16] This position is a tenable one, and the fact that Iago seizes upon ordinary motives to justify acting according to his depraved nature makes

him a subtle character indeed. "The real motive comes first—
the *invidia*. . . . If this situation suggests the word *motiveless,*
we should remember that *motiveless* is not the same as *un-
accountable* or *incomprehensible* or *meaningless.* Indeed, to
place Iago outside the circuit of commonplace cause and effect
is to make him not a lesser but an ampler character." [17] But
such a reading of the character, psychologically accurate as it
may be, goes far deeper than the surface motivation of a villain
on the stage—even on Shakespeare's stage. This subtle reading
of the play is Heilman's "approach," as he calls the opening
chapter of *Magic in the Web:* "I wish not to disparage the theater
but to argue that some writing for the theater, such as Shakespeare's, at once satisfies the requirements of the theater and
goes way beyond them; such writing provides a stage action
pleasurable to the immediate audience and at the same time
dramatic literature suitable for prolonged contemplation, indeed yielding its secrets, if it yields them, only after long study
and thought by the reader." [18] (One is reminded here of Wilson
Knight's remark on *Macbeth,* quoted in the introduction to this
book, that the subtler parts of the play can be appreciated only
after years of study.)

In my opinion, Iago's first motive, clearly set forth in the
opening lines of the play, adequately satisfies the requirements
of the theater and of the audience that expects a villain to have
a reason for his behavior. Shakespeare himself may have felt the
need for a clearly expressed motive when he reworked his source
in Cinthio's novels. In Cinthio the Ensign (Iago) is in love with
"Disdemona," the only character to whom Cinthio gives a name.
The Ensign's love is not returned, and he suspects a rival in the
Captain of the troop (Cassio). So his love turns to hate, and he
plots the death of the Captain and schemes to disrupt the love
of Disdemona and the Moor (Othello):

> Now amongst the soldiery there was an Ensign, a man of
> handsome figure, but of the most depraved nature in the
> world. This man was in great favour with the Moor, who
> had not the slightest idea of his wickedness. . . . Now the
> wicked Ensign, regardless of the faith that he had pledged
> his wife, no less than of the friendship, fidelity, and obliga-

tion which he owed the Moor, fell passionately in love with Disdemona, and bent all his thoughts to achieve his conquest. . . . the Ensign imagined that the cause of his ill success was that Disdemona loved the Captain of the troop; and he pondered how to remove him from her sight. The love which he had borne the lady now changed into the bitterest hate, and, having failed in his purposes, he devoted all his thoughts to plot the death of the Captain of the troop and to divert the affection of the Moor from Disdemona.[19]

The motivation in the source, though understandable, is not nearly so dramatic as the scene with which Shakespeare opens what has often been called his best constructed play.

The second motive, the one that has bothered thoughtful students of the play, would probably not strike the spectators as a motive at all. If they remembered Iago's soliloquy,

> I hate the Moor;
> And it is thought abroad that 'twixt my sheets
> 'Has done my office. I know not if't be true;
> Yet I, for mere suspicion in that kind,
> Will do as if for surety (I:iii:392-396),

they would think of it as the kind of suspicion that could easily rise in the mind of one already disposed toward ill will. Critics, of course, have pointed out that Iago's statement is quite out of keeping with his own characterization of Othello in such statements as "The Moor is of a free and open nature" (I:iii:405), and

> The Moor (howbeit that I endure him not)
> Is of a constant, loving, noble nature,
> And I dare think he'll prove to Desdemona
> A most dear husband. (II:i:297-300)

It was this second motive, Othello's alleged adultery with Iago's wife, Emilia, that prompted Coleridge to describe Iago's statements regarding his hatred of Othello as "the motive-hunting of motiveless malignity." [20] It does not seem to me that Coleridge's remark applies to both of Iago's motives. Its effect on subsequent criticism has, however, been significant; and this fact seems to me to be one of many examples in Shakespearean scholarship of focusing undue attention on minute flaws or in-consistencies in an otherwise convincing character. I admit that Iago's characterization might have been more convincing if this second "motive" had been left out. In commenting on the two motives Heilman vies with Coleridge's famous dictum when he writes: "What casts further doubt on the validity of these two grievances of Iago is that there are two of them. . . . Iago's case is too good; as a hunter of motives he has bagged more than the legal limit." [21] Even a third motive is just hinted at, as can be seen in Iago's soliloquy at the end of II,i:

> Now I do love her [Desdemona] too;
> Not out of absolute lust (though peradventure
> I stand accountant for as great a sin)
> But partly led to diet my revenge,
> For that I do suspect the lusty Moor
> Hath leap'd into my seat. (II:i:300-305)

It is noteworthy that the chief motive in Cinthio, Iago's un-requited love for Desdemona, is reduced to a casual reference in this scene where Iago reviews several imaginary grievances, in-cluding a suspicion of Cassio: "For I fear Cassio with my night-cap too" (II:i:316). Shakespeare may have modified Cinthio's characterization of Iago as a lover in the belief that to character-ize the cynical, intellectual Iago as motivated by unrequited love would be inconsistent with the bard's concept of this villain.

In spite of Heilman's objections, a fairer test of Iago's moti-vation might be: Would the average playgoer be disturbed by the implausibility of Iago's really believing that Othello (or Cassio) had committed adultery? And, more important, could the average playgoer fail to observe and be convinced by Iago's statement that Othello had passed him over and chosen Cassio as his lieutenant?

On another matter relating to the characterization of Iago (and Othello), the credibility of Othello's believing Iago's slan-der, I must take issue with Stoll, who finds the relation between hero and villain unconvincing: "in *Othello,* the generous and unsuspicious hero, [believes] a person whom he does not love or really know and has no right reason to trust, to the point of disbelieving persons whom he loves and has every reason to trust." [22] Here a usually reliable critic is probably in error. For Stoll to say that Othello does not "really know" Iago is, of course, literally true; yet Stoll's statement does not square with the facts as Othello understands them up to the time he is misled. After all, Iago was a subordinate of long standing; he it is to whom Othello entrusts his wife on her journey (I:iii:286); and, until Iago begins to plant unjust suspicion in the mind of his general, there is no evidence that the relation between the two has not been such as to inspire Othello's confidence in Iago. How else are we to interpret the scene in which Cassio quarrels with Roderigo and Montano and loses his lieutenancy? When Othello enters and quiets the brawling men, he turns first, not to Cassio, who is next in command, but to his trusted ensign, Iago:

> What's the matter, masters?
> Honest Iago, that looks dead with grieving,
> Speak. Who began this? On thy love, I charge thee.
>   (II:iii:176-178)

Iago is, at first, noncommittal; and Othello next questions Cassio and then Montano but without results. Angered at the evasiveness of the answers, Othello turns again to Iago and demands an explanation. After Iago has given an account *ostensibly* calculated to minimize Cassio's offense, Othello replies,

> I know, Iago,
> Thy honesty and love doth mince this matter,
> Making it light to Cassio. Cassio, I love thee;
> But never more be officer of mine.   (II:iii:246-249)

Of course, when Othello, as well as Cassio and Desdemona, keeps calling his ancient "honest Iago," the author is using dramatic irony as even the most casual spectator of the play would recognize, but human relations certainly afford many examples of this misplaced confidence; so I see no reason for regarding it as forced here.

To account for Iago's capacity to deceive, August Goll, in *Criminal Types in Shakespeare*, makes the generalization that every criminal is a cynic. He then shows how Iago fits the pattern. Starting with the passage in which Iago and Cassio discuss the charms of Desdemona (II:iii:12-29), Goll, who was no ordinary Shakespearean scholar but the chief magistrate in Aarhus, Denmark, concluded that "Iago is a cynic in his view of the relation between man and wife; and his cynicism finds repetition in his view of all other human relations and feelings." [23] Goll next considers the fascination of the cynic to honest people. Cynics are appealing because they are, in Iago's words, "nothing if not critical" (II:i:120). "Amid the interminable conventional phrases, dissimulations, half and whole lies, with which social life abounds, it is a relief to honest people to listen to one who, in this respect, seems incorruptible, one who has the courage and ability to name things by their proper names, or, at least, by names to a great extent correct. . . . Really sincere truth-seeking people, therefore, listen to [the cynic] gladly." [24] It would be hazardous to estimate what kind of person Iago (or any other complex Shakespearean character) was like before the play opens. We know that Iago was an experienced soldier, trusted by Othello and others. His critical traits may account, in some measure, for that trust which has puzzled some scholars. "Just this good-natured confidence," Goll concludes, "Iago gets from his friends. To every one he is the man who, as Cassio says, 'speaks home'. . . . His unpolished words appeal even to the refined, exalted Desdemona. . . . Iago appears to every one as the clever head, the man who knows the world and sees things clearly, who describes things as he sees them without mincing matters—the free-spoken, honest friend, bold and rough: for this reason they all seek him in their various difficulties, Desdemona, Cassio, Emilia, Roderigo." [25]

Note also—and here again I am taking issue with Professor Stoll's criticism of the plausibility of Othello's believing Iago—how realistic is the first occasion when Iago raises doubt in Othello's mind. To the question, "Was not that Cassio parted from my wife?" Iago replies:

> Cassio, my lord? No, sure, I cannot think it,
> That he would steal away so guilty-like,
> Seeing you coming. (III:iii:37-39)

Granted the malicious insinuation in the reply, the circumstances must have been most favorable for making it: Cassio had every reason to "steal away so guilty-like"; he had disgraced himself by getting into a drunken brawl and he plans to solicit Desdemona's help in petitioning for his reinstatement. No wonder he did not want to face Othello at that moment.

But the manner of Iago's insinuating remarks does not seem realistic to Stoll. He objects to Iago's "echoes and shrugs, questions and misgivings, feints and dodges, pretences and denials, and whisking of evidence under the person's nose and sticking it in his pocket." Stoll remarks: "An honest man who undertakes to tell you that . . . your wife, along with your dearest friend— has played you false, makes a clean breast of it . . . without flourish or ado." [26] Yet this is not the whole story of Iago's manner in relating his suspicions to his chief; consider the *apparent* frankness of the following:

> IAGO: I am glad of it; for now I shall have reason
> To show the love and duty that I bear you
> With franker spirit. Therefore, as I am bound,
> Receive it from me. I speak not yet of proof.
> Look to your wife; observe her well with Cassio;
> Wear your eye thus, not jealous nor secure.
> I would not have your free and noble nature,
> Out of self-bounty, be abus'd. Look to't.
> I know our country disposition well:
> In Venice they do let heaven see the pranks
> They dare not show their husbands; their best conscience
> Is not to leave't undone, but keep't unknown.
> OTHELLO: Dost thou say so?
> IAGO: She did deceive her father, marrying you;
> And when she seem'd to shake and fear your looks,
> She lov'd them most.
> OTHELLO: And so she did.
> IAGO: Why, go to then!
> She that, so young, could give out such a seeming
> To seel her father's eyes up close as oak—
> He thought 'twas witchcraft—but I am much to blame.
> I humbly do beseech you of your pardon
> For too much loving you. (III:iii:193-213)

I regard Stoll's strictures on *Othello* as examples of scholarly, historical criticism overreaching itself. Like some other modern critics, Stoll has been diligent and resourceful in trying to discover and apply to Shakespearean criticism certain conventions of the Elizabethan stage. One of these conventions was the credibility of slander. But the discovery of these conventions is a relatively minor point in criticism; the point I am trying to make is that the success or failure of Shakespeare's plays bears little relation to his observance or neglect of conventions. It could be pointed out, for instance, that Iago was a conventional villain in the eyes of Elizabethans; for Englishmen of that period looked upon Italy as a country where men indulged in intrigue for its own sake, and we can easily conceive of Elizabethans regarding Iago as an Italian who delights in villainy for the sheer pleasure he would experience in destroying so noble and powerful a general as Othello. Yet the fact that Aaron also fits several of the conventions perfectly but is not a convincing villain suggests that we must look beyond the conventions to discover what makes Iago an effective villain. First, he is made credible by his intellect and seems lifelike because of the active mind with which he is endowed and which reveals itself through his speech. He is not a villain whose decisions fluctuate so obviously in keeping with the requirements of plot as to make him seem inconsistent. Quite the contrary, the usual difficulty of trying to make both action and character appear reasonable is obviated by the clever device of having the plot seem to originate within Iago's evil mind. We tend to believe in Iago because we are fascinated by the craft and cunning he displays in his wickedness. After unsuccessfully attempting to get Othello in trouble with Brabantio for eloping with Desdemona (Act I, Scene i), his next step is to get Cassio drunk so that he will disgrace himself.

> If I can fasten but one cup upon him
> With that which he hath drunk to-night already,
> He'll be as full of quarrel and offense
> As my young mistress' dog. Now my sick fool Roderigo,
> Whom love hath turn'd almost the wrong side out,
> To Desdemona hath to-night carous'd

Potations pottle-deep; and he's to watch.
Three lads of Cyprus—noble swelling spirits,
That hold their honours in a wary distance,
The very elements of this warlike isle—
Have I to-night fluster'd with flowing cups,
And they watch too. Now, 'mongst this flock of drunkards
Am I to put our Cassio in some action
That may offend the isle. (II:iii:50-63)

As Iago had anticipated, Cassio becomes heated and quarrelsome after a few drinks; his fight with Roderigo and Montano disturbs the peace of the city, and Othello discharges him. Iago, who has cleverly engineered all this, feigns sympathy for Cassio and suggests that Othello will certainly reinstate him if he appeals to Desdemona to intercede in his behalf. Acting on this advice, Cassio makes what promises to be a successful entreaty; but, as he is leaving Desdemona, Iago enters with Othello and calls Cassio's departure to the general's attention.

> IAGO: Ha! I like not that!
> OTHELLO: What dost thou say?
> IAGO: Nothing, my lord; or if—I know not what.
> (III:iii:34-36)

The rest of this scene is devoted to a series of skillful insinuations and deliberate misinterpretations by Iago who succeeds in making Othello suspicious of his innocent wife. Once this suspicion has been aroused, Iago loses no opportunity of showing Othello further manufactured evidence of his wife's infidelity. He obtains one of Desdemona's handkerchiefs, a gift from her husband, and places it in Cassio's apartment. He has Othello listen to a conversation in which Cassio is describing his affair with a prostitute, Bianca. Othello, thinking that Cassio is alluding to Desdemona, is completely convinced of his wife's guilt and accepts Iago's suggestion that he strangle Desdemona.

For the purpose of this study, what is significant about all this action is that it does not raise the problem of harmony between plot and character that generally confronts the dramatist, especially such a dramatist as Shakespeare whose common practice was to recast old plays, modifying the action and developing and individualizing the characters to a considerable, though, as I am attempting to show, an unequal extent.

To make Iago appear well-rounded and therefore even more convincing, Shakespeare shows us several sides of his nature. While he is waiting with Cassio, Desdemona, and Emilia for Othello's arrival in Cyprus, he chides his wife humorously for talking too much.

> IAGO: [to Cassio] Sir, would she give you so much of her lips
> As of her tongue she oft bestows on me,
> You would have enough.
> DESDEMONA: Alas, she has no speech!
> IAGO: In faith, too much.
> I find it still when I have list to sleep. (II:i:101-105)

In the same scene Desdemona asks Iago how he would praise her, and there follows this bit of badinage:

> DESDEMONA: What wouldst thou write of me, if thou shouldst praise me? . . .
> IAGO: I am about it; but indeed my invention
> Comes from my pate as birdlime does from frieze . . .
> EMILIA: How if fair and foolish?
> IAGO: She never yet was foolish that was fair,
> For even her folly help'd her to an heir . . .
> DESDEMONA: O heavy ignorance! Thou praisest the worst best.
> But what praise couldst thou bestow on a deserving woman? . . .
> IAGO: She that was ever fair, and never proud;
> Had tongue at will, and yet was never loud;
> Never lack'd gold, and yet went never gay;
> Fled from her wish, and yet said 'Now I may';
> She that, being ang'red, her revenge being nigh,
> Bade her wrong stay, and her displeasure fly;
> She that in wisdom never was so frail
> To change the cod's head for the salmon's tail;
> She that could think, and ne'er disclose her mind;
> See suitors following, and not look behind:
> She was a wight (if ever such wight were)—
> DESDEMONA: To do what?
> IAGO: To suckle fools and chronicle small beer. (II:i:118-161)

Iago not only engages in these pleasantries, but also plays the hearty, convivial party man, as in the scene with Cassio and Montano where he sings drinking songs and behaves like a typical good-natured extrovert, if only we forget (as spectators must sometimes be tricked into doing) that it is all part of his skillfully constructed plan.

> CASSIO: Fore God, an excellent song!
> IAGO: I learn'd it in England, where indeed they are most potent in potting. Your Dane, your German, and your swag-bellied Hollander—Drink, ho!—are nothing to your English.
> CASSIO: Is your Englishman so expert in his drinking?
> IAGO: Why, he drinks you with facility your Dane dead drunk; he sweats not to overthrow your Almain; he gives your Hollander a vomit ere the next pottle can be fill'd.
> CASSIO: To the health of our general!
> MONTANO: I am for it, Lieutenant, and I'll do you justice.
> IAGO: O sweet England! (II:iii:77-91)

Then Iago seems to be everyone's confidant: Roderigo enlists his aid in trying to win Desdemona from Othello, Cassio plans with him how best to get back into Othello's good graces after his dismissal following the brawl, even Othello trusts Iago with his own misgivings about his wife.

One who took the time to scrutinize passages like those just quoted might argue that, except as they are necessary to the development of plot, they are extraneous and do nothing for the psychological accuracy of Iago's characterization. That would be true if we thought of Iago as villain only; but these scenes help create the illusion of reality, the belief that Iago is a real man turned villain for a purpose of his own. And so skillfully has the dramatist created this illusion that the extravagant nineteenth century praise of Shakespeare's powers of characterization, praise which seems misplaced when we try to reconcile it with a drab, uninteresting villain like Aaron, seems justifiable when applied to the lively, intellectual Iago.

III. RICHARD III, MACBETH, AND LADY MACBETH

One difficulty in evaluating the character of Shakespeare's Richard III is that varying images of the historical Richard may leave their impress on viewers of the dramatic character. Whereas spectators in the past may have found it easy to accept Shakespeare's Richard as no worse than the Richard of history, it is not easy to do so now. The concluding paragraph of an essay on Richard in *The Encyclopaedia Britannica*, for example, states the following:

> Richard was not the villain that his enemies depicted. He had good qualities, both as a man and a ruler, and showed a sound judgment of political needs. Still it is impossible to acquit him of the crime, [the murder of the young princes] the popular belief in which was the chief cause of his ruin. He was a typical man in an age of strange contradictions of character, of culture combined with cruelty, and of an emotional temper that was capable of high ends, though unscrupulous of means. Tradition represents Richard as deformed. It seems clear that he had some physical defect, though not so great as has been alleged. Extant portraits show an intellectual face characteristic of the early Renaissance, but do not indicate any deformity.[1]

Besides the problem posed by changing interpretations of the historical Richard, we have another problem unique among Shakespeare's villains: the salient features of Richard's personality begin to emerge in two earlier—and little known—plays, the second and third parts of *Henry VI*. As Spivack points out, this difficulty is minimized because "the *character* of Richard remains consistent with itself from first to last. The features of the morality convention that survive in Aaron also survive, with but slightly diminished vitality, in Richard, and project him homiletically as another exponent of the art and achievement of villainy. This is not to say that he is less vital a creation than Aaron, for the reverse is true."[2]

Richard is comparable to Aaron in some respects. According to Elizabethan psychology, both villains fall into the same classification: both appear to have lost any inclination to do right and both are perverted enough to perform their crimes without being troubled by conscience. Richard was deformed; and since audiences in Shakespeare's day (and probably until very recent times) believed that "bodily beauty signifies more good of the soul than does deformity," [3] they would recognize him and accept him even without the detailed explanation of his conduct found in his soliloquies. So far, Richard is like Aaron; but Shakespeare has raised him several steps higher on our scale of characterization. Besides the fact that he dominates his play more than any other villain except Iago and Macbeth, he is given a purpose, a past, and—most effective of all—a many-sidedness that make him appear human rather than a personification of evil introduced merely to complicate the action.

Like Edmund in *King Lear,* whose bastardy is a subject for jest, Richard has been taunted about his deformity. In *2 Henry VI* Clifford abuses Richard:

> Hence, heap of wrath, foul indigested lump,
> As crooked in thy manners as thy shape!   (V:i:157-158)

And in *3 Henry VI,* Prince Edward, before he is stabbed, insults Richard by calling him "this scolding crookback" (V:v:30), and "misshapen Dick" (V:v:35).

Richard's motive in striving to acquire the throne by force and treachery is explained in a soliloquy in *3 Henry VI:*

> Would he [King Edward] were wasted, marrow, bones, and all,
> That from his loins no hopeful branch may spring
> To cross me from the golden time I look for!
> And yet, between my soul's desire and me—
> The lustful Edward's title buried—
> Is Clarence, Henry, and his young son Edward,
> And all the unlook'd-for issue of their bodies,
> To take their rooms ere I can place myself." (III:ii:125-132)

Realizing that, with these men standing between him and his coveted throne, he does "but dream on sovereignty" (III:ii:134),

Richard considers for a moment other possibilities of fulfillment. The life of a courtier and lover he knows to be hopeless
because nature contrived

> To shrink mine arm up like a wither'd shrub;
> To make an envious mountain on my back,
> Where sits deformity to mock my body;
> To shape my legs of an unequal size;
> To disproportion me in every part. (III:ii:156-160)

His thoughts return then to his dream of the crown and suggest
the means by which he can attain it:

> Why, I can smile, and murther whiles I smile,
> And cry, 'Content!' to that which grieves my heart,
> And wet my cheeks with artificial tears,
> And frame my face to all occasions. (III:ii:182-185)

This remark explains the dissimulation he is to display in the
fourth play of the tetralogy, the one that bears his name. Here
he will indeed "set the murtherous Machiavel to school" (*3
Henry VI*, III:ii:193).

So much for the characterization of Richard before the opening of his play. In *Richard III* his personality and predicament
are summarized in the opening soliloquy where he realizes that
he is not made for times of peace.

> But I, that am not shap'd for sportive tricks
> Nor made to court an amorous looking glass;
> I, that am rudely stamp'd, and want love's majesty
> To strut before a wanton ambling nymph;
> I, that am curtail'd of this fair proportion,
> Cheated of feature by dissembling Nature,
> Deform'd, unfinish'd, sent before my time
> Into this breathing world, scarce half made up,
> And that so lamely and unfashionable
> That dogs bark at me as I halt by them—
> Why, I, in this weak piping time of peace,
> Have no delight to pass away the time,
> Unless to see my shadow in the sun
> And descant on mine own deformity.

> And therefore, since I cannot prove a lover
> To entertain these fair well-spoken days,
> I am determined to prove a villain.   (I:i:14-30)

In this passage the line, "I am determined to prove a villain," seems hardly credible to some critics who cannot conceive of anyone's admitting such a fact about himself. In my opinion, the line reads like exposition rather than characterization; and I doubt whether an audience would obect to it. Professor Stoll, however, objects to this self-analysis on Richard's part as unrealistic: "A queer creature, this, to have the gift of seeing himself as others see him, both body and soul, as hardly any one of us can do." [4] This is the type of objection that Stoll registers again and again in his strictures on the psychological accuracy of Shakespeare's characters; but in fairness to the poet's powers of characterization even in his early plays, Stoll might have pointed out the effectiveness of the whole passage in providing, like Iago's opening speech, a plausible motive for what is to follow and a reasonable explanation of Richard's perverted behavior. Though Stoll thinks otherwise,[5] I believe that Richard's soliloquy on waking from his dream in Act V is also a realistic bit of characterization. Here again Richard says, "I am a villain" (V:iii:192). Whatever shortcomings the speech as a whole may have, it seems to me psychologically accurate because Richard, having suddenly awakened from a terrifying dream in which ghosts of his victims appeared to curse him, senses in solitude and the dark of night the enormity of his crimes; and, in this momentary view of his conscience at work, we look into the depths of a lost soul.

> My conscience hath a thousand several tongues,
> And every tongue brings in a several tale,
> And every tale condemns me for a villain. . . .
> I shall despair. There is no creature loves me;
> And if I die, no soul will pity me. (V:iii:194-202)

Moving as this passage is, it is so out of keeping with Richard's usual attitude toward his crimes that even scholars can overlook it. Henry Reed, for example, assures us that "never from Richard's lips do we hear the piteous utterance of the guilt-oppressed weariness of life that weighed down the once guiltless spirit of Macbeth. Richard never felt that he had lived long enough; and, as to troops of friends, the lonely hearted and proud man set no value on them." [6]

Though it seems to me that Richard's soliloquy at the opening of the play is lifelike and that the speech just quoted shows some trace of conscience, the second scene in Act I, containing Richard's wooing of Lady Anne, certainly exceeds the limits of probability. Here, as in much of the play, Shakespeare is dealing with fact, but taking liberties with it. In the play we behold the bereaved and sorrowful Lady Anne mourning King Henry VI whose body is being carried down a London street in an open coffin. When Richard halts the procession, she rains curses on him, accusing him of the King's murder and that of her husband, Edward, Prince of Wales. Admitting his guilt, Richard offers the excuse that love for her prompted him, and then proceeds to ask her hand in marriage. She insults him in every possible way; but, before the scene is over, she accepts his ring and seems pleased at his show of penitence in desiring to participate in the funeral ceremonies for one of his victims. Although the liveliness and wit of the dialogue does much to carry this scene, it is altogether too violent to be convincing. Even Richard seems to recognize this; note the lines: "Was ever woman in this humour woo'd?/Was ever woman in this humour won" (I:ii:227-228)? It is a conspicuous and unforgettable scene even to the casual spectator; because of its prominent position at the opening of the play, it sets a tone of unreality and implausibility. We noticed a similar flaw in *Titus Andronicus* where the atrocities on both sides at the beginning of the play marked it as a drama in which sensational violence was emphasized at the expense of lifelike characterization. Richard's wooing of Anne should be contrasted with the opening scene in *Othello* where Iago begrudges Cassio his promotion and blames Othello for not rewarding him with the lieutenancy. That scene sets the tone of truth to life which subsequent minor inconsistencies and implausibilities do little to vitiate. In *Richard III*, unfortunately, the situation is reversed. Though, as the play proceeds, we come to accept the effects of Richard's hypocrisy on others,

this first instance of it is unconvincing. If we could have had
the scene at the close of Act III without the wooing of Anne,
Richard's characterization might have seemed more convincing.
In that later scene few spectators could fail to be impressed by
the irony of the Lord Mayor and Buckingham's interrupting
Richard, Duke of Gloucester, at his prayers and urging on the
seemingly unwilling hypocrite the crown of England.

> MAYOR: See where his Grace stands, 'tween two clergymen.
> BUCKINGHAM: Two props of virtue for a Christian prince . . .
> And see, a book of prayer in his hand,
> True ornaments to know a holy man.
> Famous Plantagenet, most gracious prince,
> Lend favourable ear to our requests,
> And pardon us the interruption
> Of thy devotion and right Christian zeal.
> RICHARD: My lord, there needs no such apology.
> I do beseech your Grace to pardon me,
> Who, earnest in the service of my God,
> Deferr'd the visitation of my friends.
> But, leaving this, what is your Grace's pleasure?
>
>   (III:vii:95-108)

Buckingham then tells Richard that he should accept the
"throne majestical" now in the hands of "blemish'd stock" under
whose rule England is "defac'd with scars of infamy" (III:vii:118-
126). Richard pretends to disagree about the quality of the in-
cumbent, insisting that

> The royal tree hath left us royal fruit,
> Which, mellow'd by the stealing hours of time,
> Will well become the seat of majesty. (III:vii:167-169)

Though his refusal of the proffered crown seems definite when
he implores the Mayor and Buckingham not to "heap this care
on me" (III:vii:204), he has them called back just as they are
leaving and announces that he will unwillingly accept:

> Cousin of Buckingham, and sage grave men,
> Since you will buckle fortune on my back,
> To bear her burthen, whe'r I will or no,
> I must have patience to endure the load. (III:vii:227-230)

Here as elsewhere Richard's vitality springs from his perfect hypocrisy; or, paradoxical as it may sound, he appears real because he is so obviously—and so cleverly—playing a part. In this quality he resembles Iago; he is also like Iago in his vivaciousness. As Dowden says:

> [Richard] is not a gloomy villain; the laws of the world being inverted for him, he lives with a certain glee in this inverted world. An actor has not caught Shakespeare's idea unless he can play the part—as did Irving—with a kind of perverted gaiety, and a smiling contempt for his victims.[7]

We see an example of that "smiling contempt" in Act III, Scene v, when the head of Hastings, whom Richard has ordered executed for treason, is brought in.

> LOVEL: Here is the head of that ignoble traitor,
> The dangerous and unsuspected Hastings.
> RICHARD: So dear I lov'd the man, that I must weep.
> I took him for the plainest harmless creature
> That breath'd upon the earth a Christian;
> Made him my book, wherein my soul recorded
> The history of all her secret thoughts.
> So smooth he daub'd his vice with show of virtue
> That, his apparent open guilt omitted—
> I mean, his conversation with Shore's wife—
> He liv'd from all attainder of suspect. (III:v:22-32)

We also see his perverted gaiety at work when he attempts to comfort the Duchess of York, following the death of Clarence who has been killed at Richard's command.

> DUCHESS: God bless thee, and put meekness in thy breast,
> Love, charity, obedience, and true duty!
> RICHARD: Amen!—[aside] and make me die a good old man!
> That is the butt end of a mother's blessing.
> I marvel that her Grace did leave it out. (II:ii:107-111)

In praising the characterization of Richard, I would not go so far as did Steevens who claimed that

> The part of Richard is, perhaps, beyond all others, variegated, and consequently favorable to a judicious performer. It comprehends, indeed, a trait of almost every species of

character on the stage. The hero, the lover, the statesman, the buffoon, the hypocrite, the hardened and repenting sinner, &c., are to be found within its compass. No wonder, therefore, that the discriminating powers of a Burbage, a Garrick, and a Henderson, should at different periods have given it a popularity beyond other dramas of the same author.[8]

There is, of course, some truth in what Steevens has written, yet there is one quality lacking that we have still to discover in any of the villains thus far discussed. That is remorse. Although, as we have shown on page fifty above, remorse is not totally lacking in Richard, it is by no means a dominant trait. In contrasting Macbeth with Richard, we shall find remorse and sensitivity in ample measure.

Of the twenty excerpts under the heading "On the Character of Richard" printed in the *New Variorum Shakespeare*,[9] eight passages compare Richard III with Macbeth. Richard is also compared with Milton's Satan, with Iago, Edmund, Lady Macbeth, and Shylock. But the comparison with Macbeth is the most natural; and the most detailed and discerning comparison with Macbeth is taken from Thomas Whately's *Remarks on Some of the Characters of Shakespeare*. Whately recognizes the similarity in situation between Richard and Macbeth: both villains are soldiers and usurpers, both attain their throne by regicide and treason, both lose their lives in battle against the men who claim to be lawful heirs.

The supernatural fables surrounding Richard and Macbeth are significant in accounting for their motivation. The tyranny of Richard was foretold by omens attending his birth, omens suggesting that he was vicious by nature. Shakespeare also makes use of the legend concerning Richard's deformity to account for his natural depravity and to provide a motive. By way of contrast, the prophesies of the witches come after Macbeth has led a decent, honorable life. What ambitions he had prior to his temptation were presumably lawful and kept within bounds. If he had not been tempted by the witches, a temptation difficult to resist because of the proddings of his wife, Macbeth's character might have deterred him from murder.

The omens surrounding the lives of the two villains are matched by their dispositions. Macbeth is characterized as sensitive. He is reluctant to commit murder because he has the natural feelings of gratitude and hospitality toward Duncan. The fact that he worries over the prophecy in favor of Banquo's issue is taken by Whately to indicate the envy he feels toward his rival. This envy is based on an understandable desire to have his offspring continue on the throne. In brief, there is some tenderness in Macbeth's makeup, a tenderness almost totally lacking in Richard. "I, that have neither pity, love, nor fear" (*3 Hen. VI*, V:vi:68), is the statement with which Richard characterizes himself.

If Macbeth is sensitive and remorseful, indulgence in crime seems to be part of Richard's nature. Before King Henry VI is murdered, he tells Richard:

> The owl shriek'd at thy birth, an evil sign;
> The night crow cried, aboding luckless time;
> Dogs howl'd and hideous tempest shook down trees;
> The raven rook'd her on the chimney top,
> And chatt'ring pies in dismal discord sung.
> Thy mother felt more than a mother's pain,
> And yet brought forth less than a mother's hope,
> To wit, an indigested and deformed lump,
> Not like the fruit of such a goodly tree.
> Teeth hadst thou in thy head when thou wast born,
> To signify thou cam'st to bite the world.
> > (*3 Hen. VI*, V:vi:44-54)

Richard seems not at all troubled by the king's accusation. He replies, while stabbing the king, "For this (amongst the rest) was I ordain'd" (V:vi:57). A few lines later he seems resigned to the fact and even proud that the omens attending his birth are being justified in his conduct.

> Then, since the heavens have shap'd my body so,
> Let hell make crook'd my mind to answer it.
> I have no brother, I am like no brother;
> And this word 'love,' which greybeards call divine,
> Be resident in men like one another,
> And not in me! I am myself alone. (V:vi:78-83)

If crimes come naturally to Richard, Macbeth is agonized by the thought of them. Macbeth speaks of the "heat-oppressed brain" (II:i:39), and, after having committed murder, he says he is "afraid to think what I have done" (II:ii:51). Macbeth's temperament undoubtedly strikes an audience as more lifelike than that of Richard, who reveals a perverted gaiety whenever he contemplates, executes, or reflects upon his most desperate crimes. Upon parting from his brother Clarence, who is being led off to prison, Richard says:

> Simple plain Clarence! I do love thee so
> That I will shortly send thy soul to heaven,
> If heaven will take the present at our hands.   (I:i:118-120)

And two acts later while meditating the murder of his nephews, he applies proverbs with a bitter irony: "So wise so young, they say do never live long" (III:i:79), and "Short summers lightly have a forward spring" (III:i:94). If Macbeth is sensitive to the good qualities in his monarch, Richard ridicules such virtues as signs of weakness. After he has killed King Henry VI, Richard remarks, "See how my sword weeps for the poor King's death" (*3 Hen. VI*, V:vi:63). And later when Lady Anne, accusing Richard of the king's murder, exclaims, "O, he was gentle, mild, and virtuous," Richard's sardonic reply is, "The better for the King of Heaven, that hath him" (I:ii:104-105).

Macbeth is stricken by remorse over his deeds; he also fails to enjoy the fruits of his crimes. Although he once calls himself "high-plac'd Macbeth" (IV:i:98), he does not enjoy his advancement, especially since it is not attended with respect. We cannot imagine Richard wasting much time worrying over the lack of respect and love shown him by his subjects—except in one memorable scene. "I am myself alone," seems to be the line most frequently cited by commentators in the *Variorum* to characterize Richard.

The difficulty that Macbeth has in acting a part contrary to his better nature is cited by Whately as being in striking contrast to Richard's life, which is compounded of an easily assumed hypocrisy and dissimulation. The trouble that Macbeth's conscience causes him, especially in the banquet scene, cannot but strike the reader as lifelike, whereas Richard's gleeful hypocrisy seems unnatural and diabolical.

Whately's comparison between Richard III and Macbeth, which I have summarized above, attempts to show Shakespeare's "excellence in distinguishing characters." Whately picks these two murderers because, as he so well shows, "none seem to agree so much in situation, and to differ so much in disposition, as RICHARD THE THIRD and MACBETH." [10]

In a recent book, *Shakespeare and the Allegory of Evil*, Bernard Spivack divides these two villains in a different way: "Richard belongs to 'The Family of Iago.' He is at once a dramatic character based upon an historical monarch, and a carryover of the Vice from the morality play, a type character who lingered into the early Elizabethan period." Spivack's characterization of Richard is ingenious if somewhat sweeping, as he admits:

> How distinctly these four [Aaron, Richard III, Don John, and Iago] qualify as members of a special genre becomes even more evident when they are compared with Shakespeare's other criminals. Against them a Claudius, an Angelo, a Goneril, a Macbeth, a Iachimo, even Shylock and Cymbeline's Queen, are cogent portraits of humanity. They are verbally and emotionally consistent, and their behavior is morally perspicuous. Their motives exist incontestably and are pertinent, specific, continuous, and logically directed to fulfillment. They respond to temptations and provocations that are valid results of the interplay between their natures and the circumstances of their lives." [11]

The chief value of Spivack's argument lies in its showing a historical continuity between a medieval type character, the Vice, and the more or less logically motivated villain that gradually replaced him. Spivack's argument does not vitiate my contention that a villain on the stage will be accepted or rejected by the audience in proportion to his truth to life and his obvious motives. And collaterally, the success or failure of the play may depend upon the skill with which the author has endowed him with obvious and apparent motives. I do find Spivack's classification useful, and the fact that he places Richard III in one camp and Macbeth in another certainly makes sense.

So far we have considered Macbeth mainly in relation to Richard III. Before making a final evaluation of Macbeth's characterization, we should consider him vis-à-vis Lady Macbeth. *Macbeth* is the second play we have considered in which more than one villain has a part. Like Tamora in *Titus Andronicus,* Lady Macbeth seems at first to be the stronger of the two villains. Since Macbeth is characterized as a good man at the beginning of the play, Shakespeare's problem is to present him as sorely tempted by the forces of evil (the witches), by the fate that brings Duncan to spend the night as his guest, and, most of all, by his wife. Certainly audiences in this or any other age would understand that a man's ambition—lawful or unlawful—might be stimulated and shared by his wife. She lives for him and for his success. So what could be more plausible than characterizing Lady Macbeth as spurring on her husband's ambition, ignoble though it be? We do not have to believe that Lady Macbeth is actually as unwomanly or as fiendish as some of her outbursts suggest. We can understand those speeches as the goadings of a wife determined to advance her husband at whatever cost to herself and to him. If we look at Lady Macbeth in this light, as a character who serves as a foil to her husband, most of the problems regarding her "real nature" will be resolved. Much ink has been spilled over the question of Lady Macbeth's character. Mrs. Jameson summarizes the problem well in *Shakespeare's Female Characters:*

> In the play or poem of Macbeth, the interest of the story is so engrossing, the events so rapid and so appalling, the accessories so sublimely conceived and so skillfully combined, that it is difficult to detach Lady Macbeth from the dramatic situation, or consider her apart from the terrible associations of our first and earliest impressions . . . the common place idea of Lady Macbeth . . . is nothing but a fierce, cruel woman, brandishing a couple of daggers, and inciting her husband to butcher a poor old king. . . . generally speaking, the commentators seem to have considered Lady Macbeth rather with reference to her husband, as influenc-

ing the action of the drama, than as an individual concep-
tion of amazing power, poetry and beauty.[12]

Mrs. Jameson then goes on to take issue with such typical interpretations as those of Johnson and Schlegel, who regard Lady
Macbeth as little more than an ogress or "species of female
fury." [13] Her analysis makes an interesting, if somewhat fanci-
ful, character sketch of Lady Macbeth; but I think she comes
closest to the truth in the passage quoted above where she points
to the difficulty of detaching Lady Macbeth from the dramatic
situation. Granted that Lady Macbeth may be conceived of as
a character in her own right, worthy of the many essays written
about her, she is, first and foremost, an accessory to her husband.
It is Macbeth's play; it is he who first thinks of murdering the
king and who carries out that crime and those which follow.
It is erroneous, I believe, to state, as Schlegel did, that: "Little
more than the mere execution of Duncan falls to the share of
Macbeth." [14] Once Macbeth is launched on his career of murder, he proceeds with little help from his wife.

How then should we look at the character of Lady Macbeth?
Although she has the second longest part in the play, she is
given only about one-third as many lines as her husband; and
after the banquet scene in Act III, she is not heard from again
until Act V. Her function at the beginning of the play is partly
expository; we understand Macbeth better through her. When
she reads the letter in which Macbeth greets her as "my dearest
partner of greatness" and in which he tells her something "of
what greatness is promis'd thee" (I:v:13-14), the audience understands the ambition shared by the pair. Lady Macbeth is also
characterized early in the play as a foil to her husband, as one
who understands and fears his reluctance to carry through the
desperate enterprise on which they are embarked, and as one
who will counterbalance his hesitation with her own ruthless
determination. We learn about Macbeth's character through
Lady Macbeth's speeches, as in the following:

> Yet do I fear thy nature.
> It is too full o' th' milk of human kindness
> To catch the nearest way. Thou wouldst be great;

> Art not without ambition, but without
> The illness should attend it. What thou wouldst highly,
> That wouldst thou holily. . . .
>   Hie thee hither,
> That I may pour my spirits in thine ear
> And chastise with the valour of my tongue
> All that impedes thee from the golden round
> Which fate and metaphysical aid doth seem
> To have thee crown'd withal. (I:v:17-31)

May it not be that, in trying to establish the good qualities in
Macbeth early in the play, Shakespeare had to sacrifice complexity and even plausibility in the lesser character of Lady Macbeth? Or looked at another way, may not the actual words of
Lady Macbeth when she is trying to spur on her husband be
discounted by the audience that sees chiefly the truth-to-life of
the principle revealed by her speeches, that an ambitious and
unscrupulous wife will go to any extremes to advance her husband? When Macbeth begins to waver in his purpose, she goads
him on and shames him into action:

>   Was the hope drunk
> Wherein you dress'd yourself? Hath it slept since?
> And wakes it now to look so green and pale
> At what it did so freely? From this time
> Such I account thy love. Art thou afeard
> To be the same in thine own act and valour
> As thou art in desire? . . .
>   What beast was't then
> That made you break this enterprise to me?
> When you durst do it, then you were a man. (I:vii:35-49)

Lady Macbeth's will is strong throughout the first acts of
the play. In fact, the general opinion, as mentioned above, is
that she is inhumanly strong and even fiendish. Such lines as the
following have often been quoted to support this interpretation:

> I have given suck, and know
> How tender 'tis to love the babe that milks me.
> I would, while it was smiling in my face,
> Have pluck'd my nipple from his boneless gums

And dash'd the brains out, had I so sworn as you
Have done to this. (I:vii:54-59)

There is no doubt that Lady Macbeth's language in this passage might lead an audience to regard her as fiendish, but note the following interpretation by Coleridge:

> A passage where she alludes to "plucking her nipple from the boneless gums of her infant," though usually thought to prove a merciless and unwomanly nature, proves the direct opposite: she brings it as the most solemn enforcement to Macbeth of the solemnity of his promise to undertake the plot against Duncan. Had *she* so sworn, she would have done that which was most horrible to her feelings, rather than break the oath; and as the most horrible act which it was possible for imagination to conceive, . . . she alludes to the destruction of her infant, while in the act of sucking at her breast. Had she regarded this with savage indifference, there would have been no force in the appeal; but her very allusion to it, and her purpose in this allusion, shows that she considered no tie so tender as that which connected her with her babe.[15]

Although the first and strongest impression of Lady Macbeth remains that of a hardhearted, ruthless woman, on at least two occasions in the second act Shakespeare presents her with typically feminine qualities. She cannot murder Duncan because she sees in the sleeping monarch a resemblance to her own father:

> Had he not resembled
> My father as he slept, I had done't. (II:ii:13-14)

Later in the same act, when Lady Macbeth hears that the grooms of Duncan's chamber have also been murdered, she faints. Critics have differed as to whether her action is feigned or real. I agree with Bradley that a stronger case can be made for the fainting's being real.[16] If she had been acting, she probably would have fainted when the murder of Duncan was announced. But these additional murders surprise her; she is not prepared for them; and she reveals her womanly nature by fainting. Except for these two indications of femininity, however, Lady Macbeth's character remains resolute throughout Act III, Scene iv, the scene in which the ghost of Banquo appears to haunt Macbeth. After that scene her part in the plot is finished; she has fulfilled her purpose, which is to spur Macbeth on to his first murder and to help him try to conceal his guilt during the banquet scene. It is true that the sleep-walking scene of Act V is one of the high moments in the play. It may be regarded as a remarkable exhibition of the workings of conscience, as a revelation of the terrible penalty for Lady Macbeth's part in the crime, or as an attempt on Shakespeare's part to modify the essentially heartless characterization of Lady Macbeth earlier in the play. Henry Crabb Robinson has the following comment:

> It however occurs to me that this sleep-walking is perhaps the vindication of Shakespeare in his portraiture of the character [Lady Macbeth] . . . while the voluntary actions and sentiments of Lady M. are all inhuman, her involuntary nature rises against her habitual feelings springing out of depraved passions, and in her sleep she shews to be a woman, while waking she is a monster.[17]

Modern critics would find in her downfall a fine bit of irony: Lady Macbeth, whose character seems so resolute at the beginning of the play, loses control of herself, not during her waking hours, but in her sleep. And the woman who spurs her husband on to murder the sleeping Duncan suffers the tortures of remorse in her sleep. But interest in Lady Macbeth, so far as plot is concerned, diminishes after the banquet scene. Macbeth is only momentarily moved at the report of her death: "She should have died hereafter;/There would have been a time for such a word" (V:v:17-18). In the final scene of the play we are left in doubt as to just how Lady Macbeth died. Malcolm reports that " 'tis thought, by self and violent hands [she]/Took off her life" (V:viii:70-71).

If the characterization of Lady Macbeth is somewhat sketchily drawn, that of her husband is much more fully developed. When one compares Macbeth with the Machiavellian Richard III, he finds a good example of the development in Shakespeare's powers of characterization. Kittredge dates *Macbeth* about 1606, fourteen years later than *Richard III;* [18] in the space of these years one can measure the extent of Shakespeare's growing interest in psychological accuracy of character portrayal. As for the earlier play, my analysis of it has, I hope, borne out E. K. Chambers' statement that "the psychology [of Richard III] is 'primitive'. . . . It is in the key and at the distance from life of melodrama, not tragedy. . . . The concentrated remorselessness of Richard recalls [Marlowe]." [19]

If the psychology of Richard is primitive, the characterization of Macbeth is of the greatest subtlety. No less a critic than A. C. Bradley states that "psychologically it is perhaps the most remarkable exhibition of the *development* of a character to be found in Shakespeare's tragedies." [20] What distinguishes Macbeth from all other Shakespearean villains is the evidence of nobility in his nature, a quality that reveals itself in the remorse he feels for his crimes. Certainly there is little enough of that quality in Richard, and none in Iago. Probably in no other Shakespearean villain do we feel that so much potential good is subverted to evil. And whereas, in watching the villainy of Iago or Richard, we are awed by their ingenuity in engineering the destruction of their victims, this fascination is not present in *Macbeth*. Here we are moved by the spectacle of disintegration in this hero-villain, for Macbeth destroys himself. His ambition may be divided into two parts: in the first part of the play we see him tempted and trying to struggle against his ambition; in the second we see him, having abandoned himself to evil, suffering from the realization of what he is doing.

In whatever light we regard the witches—as the forces of evil in the world tempting a good man to his ruin, or as symbolic representations of Macbeth's inner struggle—the first act of the play presents the spectacle of a potentially great man succumbing to evil. Bradley thinks that Macbeth was not entirely innocent even at the time he heard the first prophecies because "no innocent man would have started, as he did, with a start of *fear* at the mere prophecy of a crown, or have conceived thereupon *immediately* the thought of murder." [21] We are not told what ambitions, vague or definite, Macbeth may have entertained before the play opens; [22] but it is clear that the prompt fulfillment of part of the witches' prophecy—his being made

Thane of Cawdor—kindles unlawful desires in Macbeth's mind:

> [Aside] This supernatural soliciting
> Cannot be ill; cannot be good. If ill,
> Why hath it given me earnest of success,
> Commencing in a truth? I am Thane of Cawdor.
> If good, why do I yield to that suggestion
> Whose horrid image doth unfix my hair
> And make my seated heart knock at my ribs
> Against the use of nature?   (I:iii:130-137)

He then expresses the hope that he may become king without having to engage in crime: "If chance will have me King, why, chance may crown me,/Without my stir" (I:iii:142-143). As Boyer says in *The Villain as Hero in Elizabethan Tragedy,*

> When Macbeth decided to leave all to chance he was in di-rect line to succeed to the throne; he had only to await the old king's death. But in Scene 4 [of Act I] . . . the king desig-nates Malcolm his heir. Chance has put a block in Macbeth's way and he at once decides to trust to chance no longer.[23]

We next see Macbeth's unlawful ambitions stirred when Duncan announces that "We will establish our estate upon/Our eldest, Malcolm" (I:iv:37-38). This remark prompts another aside by Macbeth:

> The Prince of Cumberland! that is a step
> On which I must fall down, or else o'erleap,
> For in my way it lies. Stars, hide your fires!
> Let not light see my black and deep desires.
> The eye wink at the hand; yet let that be,
> Which the eye fears, when it is done, to see.   (I:iv:48-53)

In *Shakespeare Today* Margaret Webster points out that Shake-speare's sources provide adequate motivation for Macbeth's vil-lainy.

> His source book, the *Chronicles* of Holinshed, gives plenty of facts from which he might have built up a case for the Macbeths, had he wished to do so. For instance, Macbeth was Duncan's cousin, and, since the Crown of Scotland did not at that time descend by right to the King's eldest son, he

had every right to suppose that he would be elected to the throne after Duncan's death. The old man's attempt to "establish our estate upon our eldest, Malcolm," was, in fact, highly unconstitutional. There was the further consideration, not altogether trivial, that Macbeth's father, and Lady Macbeth's grandfather, brother, and first husband had all been slain in varying circumstances of treachery and violence by Duncan's unamiable predecessor, Malcolm the Second. Between the two houses there was, accordingly, a blood-feud of long standing. But Macbeth had served Duncan loyally and with great ability.[24]

But if Shakespeare had emphasized the motivation furnished in the source to show that Macbeth had some just reason to expect the kingship, the play and the character would have been different. Instead, Shakespeare shows us a good man tempted without having been wronged by his king, as he was in Holinshed. Quite the contrary, Macbeth feels an obligation to Duncan.

During the scene in which Lady Macbeth reads her husband's letter about his newly-acquired title and the even greater position prophesied, it becomes clear that, though Macbeth has great ambitions, his wife fears that he may be too scrupulous to realize them unlawfully. From the time when the temptation of Duncan's visit begins to corrupt Macbeth, Lady Macbeth takes the initiative in bringing about the first crime. Macbeth's good intentions are no match for the urgings of his unlawful ambition spurred on by his wife. Here, if anywhere, the reflective spectator might find something unconvincing in Macbeth's characterization because, in spite of the seemingly forthright nature of his two objections:

> We will proceed no further in this business.
> He hath honour'd me of late, and I have bought
> Golden opinions from all sorts of people,
> Which would be worn now in their newest gloss,
> Not cast aside so soon,

and

> Prithee peace!
> I dare do all that may become a man.
> Who dares do more is none   (I:vii:31-47),

he soon yields to the importunings of his wife. Yet, in this especially swift-moving play—*Macbeth* is only half as long as *Hamlet*
and much shorter than the other two great tragedies—Macbeth's
speed in yielding would probably not seem unconvincing. In fact,
the compactness and clarity with which, in a single short act, are
revealed the various agencies that lead a man to crime—his ambition, the placing of temptations in his path, the urgings of his
wife, and the strange prophecies of the witches that an audience
in earlier times would probably accept as the work of the devil,
but that present-day audiences would understand as symbolizing
the impersonal force of evil in the world—tend to make Macbeth's fall seem realistic.

It now remains to examine the subsequent course of the play
in which the original crime leads Macbeth, not to any enjoyment
of his usurped position such as Claudius apparently experienced,
but to a feeling of increasing insecurity and despair amounting
at times to panic. This change in Macbeth commands our interest
because people tend to regard a criminal more sympathetically
if he is represented as suffering remorse for his misdeeds. In this
respect Macbeth certainly claims our sympathetic attention.

The ambivalence of Macbeth, observed in the first act when
he vacillates between a desire to gain his unlawful ambition and
an awareness of the enormity of his proposed crime, reveals itself
in a different form in the subsequent acts. For example, in his
instructions to the murderers of Banquo, Macbeth is for the moment the calculating, scheming villain insinuating that Banquo
is the murderers' cold-blooded enemy:

> Well then, now
> Have you consider'd of my speeches? Know
> That it was he, in the times past, which held you
> So under fortune.   (III:i:75-78)

But at the banquet he is frightened by the appearance of
Banquo's ghost, and his wife's presence of mind is required to
keep Macbeth from revealing his guilt. After the guests have been
dismissed, Macbeth determines to visit the weird sisters; for,

> now I am bent to know
> By the worst means the worst. For mine own good

All causes shall give way. I am in blood
Stepp'd in so far that, should I wade no more,
Returning were as tedious as go o'er.
Strange things I have in head, that will to hand,
Which must be acted ere they may be scann'd.
    (III:iv:134-140)

After the second interview with the witches, Macbeth's character disintegrates rapidly; and in Act IV he has Lady Macduff and her children savagely slaughtered. This is similar to the villainy of Aaron and Richard with the significant difference that, whereas one could conceive of Aaron and probably Richard as capable of instigating such atrocities at any point in their careers, such behavior belongs only to the fallen Macbeth. Macbeth realizes how he has changed; and there are two memorable utterances in which he characterizes himself:

I have liv'd long enough. My way of life
Is fall'n into the sere, the yellow leaf;
And that which should accompany old age,
As honour, love, obedience, troops of friends,
I must not look to have; but, in their stead,
Curses not loud but deep, mouth-honour, breath,
Which the poor heart would fain deny, and dare not,
    (V:iii:22-28)

and

I have almost forgot the taste of fears.
The time has been, my senses would have cool'd
To hear a night-shriek, and my fell of hair
Would at a dismal treatise rouse and stir
As life were in't. I have supp'd full with horrors.
Direness, familiar to my slaughterous thoughts,
Cannot once start me.   (V:v:9-15)

Psychologically, then, the description of Macbeth's moral fiber breaking under the pressure of temptation, the revelation of a once noble character succumbing to overpowering ambition, is a superb piece of characterization. But if we consider his character dramatically and try to appraise him as a part of the whole play, there will be several questions to ponder. In the first place, the characterization of Macbeth leaves some doubt as to whether the outcome of the play is tragic. The play is called a tragedy, and we witness in it the downfall of a potentially noble man; yet in Macbeth's death we see the triumph of good over evil. Another problem is the role of Macbeth as protagonist or hero of the play. We have already noted that our sympathy and understanding were directed toward him. This means that the good people in the play, Malcolm and Donalbain, Macduff and his family, who are engaged in combatting evil and who should command our sympathy, tend to be slighted. As Dr. Maginn said:

> We feel no more interest in the gracious Duncan, in Banquo, in Lady Macduff, than we do in the slaughtered grooms. . . . The other characters of the play, with the exception of the two principal, are nonentities. We care nothing for Malcolm or Donalbain, or Lenox or Rosse, or the rest of the Scottish nobles.[25]

Factors such as these weaken the play dramatically; consequently it appears that the characterization of Macbeth, like that of Shylock, whom we shall consider in the next chapter, is too accurate psychologically to fit in neatly as one of the component parts of a drama. Taken by itself as a psychological study, it is admirable; but as a part of what should be a dramatic unity, it raises certain doubts. Normally Macbeth would have been the villain, and someone else the hero of the play. But the growing tendency in Shakespeare's development to justify the villain in terms of human psychology has gone so far that the villain has become the hero, the person in whom, at the beginning and end, we are chiefly interested and with whom we sympathize.

IV. ANGELO AND SHYLOCK

Angelo and Shylock are villains in comedies, villains who attempt crimes but whose villainy is thwarted. Even so, we can evaluate them according to criteria established for the other villains. The danger of putting too much faith in the recently emphasized conventions of the Elizabethan stage can be illustrated by examining criticism of Angelo in *Measure for Measure*. If we accept the convention that a "sudden repentance of the villain is . . . never convincing, but it is never to be questioned," [1] we are dodging a crux in the interpretation of Angelo's character. For it is just that point, his sudden repentance, that the critics argue.

One school of thought, prominent at least since Coleridge's time, holds that the repentance of Angelo is out of character and that his marriage to Mariana and subsequent pardon provide an unsatisfactory ending. According to Coleridge,

> This play, which is Shakespeare's throughout, is to me the most painful—say rather, the only painful—part of his genuine works. . . . the pardon and marriage of Angelo not merely baffles the strong indignant claim of justice (for cruelty, with lust and damnable baseness, cannot be forgiven, because we cannot conceive them as being *morally* repented of) but it is likewise degrading to the character of woman. [2]

Swinburne regards the ending as a concession to what would have been aesthetically and dramatically appropriate to the conventional demands of comedy. He calls it a "sacrifice of moral beauty or spiritual harmony to the necessities and traditions of the stage." He explains it as follows:

> It will be observed that the sacrifice is made to comedy. The actual or hypothetical necessity of pairing off all the couples after such a fashion as to secure a nominally happy and undeniably matrimonial ending is the theatrical idol whose tyranny exacts this holocaust of higher and better feelings. [3]

It is interesting to compare the attitudes of these two critics. Following his own advice, Coleridge "exercises that willing suspension of disbelief . . . that constitutes poetic faith." The play becomes painful for him because he confuses make-believe with reality. He regards Angelo and Isabella as real persons: a villain whose pardon thwarts the demands of justice, and a woman whose marriage to this villain degrades her character. Apparently he does not read this play thematically; therefore he does not see these two characters as symbols of justice and mercy. Swinburne's objection is on aesthetic grounds. He sees the play as a play, but one in which the artificial and theatrical requirements of comedy take precedence over a resolution of the action appropriate to the demands of high seriousness.

Both these critics agree in disapproving the way Shakespeare handles his material. More recently, however, there have been critics who see in Angelo not base villainy, but justice and intellect in operation. An extreme view is that of W. M. T. Dodds, who rejects the common views that Angelo is "either a dissembler or a prig and sees him as a man whose soul is large and fine enough to experience tragic intensity of suffering."

> Shakespeare has taken great care to show Angelo as a man whose ideals of abstract Justice are clear, and to be revered, whatever his own practice as a "justicer" may be. To dismiss these ideals as narrow, priggish, pharisaical, is to destroy the dramatic antithesis upon which the argument turns. It is therefore vital to the understanding of the play as a whole to put from oneself all hostility to the idea of Justice as typified by Angelo before his fall. It is a Christian commonplace to think of justice giving place to mercy, but it is unchristian to decry justice itself.[4]

There are two fallacies in the argument: however neatly Shakespeare may or may not have contrived the antithesis between justice and mercy and however much all of us should respect the ideal of justice, few audiences in Shakespeare's or any other age could reconcile the proposed execution of Claudio with the notion of justice. Even an audience receptive to Angelo's concept of justice cannot help but regard as hypocritical a man who

argues so convincingly about justice *after* he has treated Mariana
so unfairly. When he offers Isabella so monstrous a solution to
her brother's difficulties, he goes beyond hypocrisy and proposes
to commit the very crime for which his brand of justice claims
Claudio's life.

Although Dodd's position is extreme, there is some evidence
that Shakespeare intended to represent Angelo not as a base villain, but as a man who succumbs to temptation. When the Duke
proposes to make Angelo his deputy, Escalus, an ancient Lord,
says that if anyone in Vienna is worthy of such honor, it is
Angelo. The Duke himself praises Angelo as follows:

> There is a kind of character in thy life
> That to th'observer doth thy history
> Fully unfold. Thyself and thy belongings
> Are not thine own so proper as to waste
> Thyself upon thy virtues, they on thee.
> Heaven doth with us as we with torches do,
> Not light them for themselves; for if our virtues
> Did not go forth of us, 'twere all alike
> As if we had them not. Spirits are not finely touch'd
> But to fine issues; nor Nature never lends
> The smallest scruple of her excellence
> But, like a thrifty goddess, she determines
> Herself the glory of a creditor,
> Both thanks and use.   (I:i:28-41)

Perhaps, as in the characterization of Iago, this is intended as
dramatic irony. But there are several objections to this interpretation. First, though the Duke speaks highly of Angelo in naming
him his deputy, he is in fact testing the man, as can be seen by
the Duke's remark to Friar Thomas at the close of Act I, Scene iii:

> Lord Angelo is precise,
> Stands at a guard with envy, scarce confesses
> That his blood flows or that his appetite
> Is more to bread than stone; hence shall we see,
> If power change purpose, what our seemers be.
>   (I:iii:50-54)

Note that in this speech, as in Lucio's of I:iv:57-61, the nature of
Angelo's character is more specifically defined. He is an austere,

ascetic type; he is certainly not magnanimous or generous. The Duke is already aware of certain shortcomings in his character, as we see in Act III, Scene i, where the Duke explains to Isabella that, because Mariana's dowry was accidentally lost, Angelo refused to marry her. Instead, he "left her in tears and dried not one of them with his comfort; swallowed his vows whole, pretending in her discoveries of dishonour" (III:i:234-237). This is certainly no indication of the spotless character that the Duke pays tribute to in the first passage cited above. It reveals, instead, a man compounded of strength and weakness; if we look at Angelo's prototypes in Shakespeare's sources, we see what modifications the dramatist has made to lend credibility to Angelo. In *Shakespeare's Sources I, Comedies and Tragedies,* Kenneth Muir describes some sources that Shakespeare may have used.

In Cinthio's *Hecatommithi* Juriste (Angelo) is left by the Emperor to govern Innsbruck. Vico (Claudio) is condemned to die, not for fornication, but for rape. His sister Epitia (Isabella) begs Juriste to pardon her brother, and the deputy agrees to do so if Epitia will sleep with him. After some urging and the suggestion that he may marry her, she consents; but Juriste has Vico executed and sends the body to his sister. Thus betrayed, Epitia complains to the Emperor. To compensate for the wrong he has done Epitia, Juriste is forced to marry her and is sentenced to die immediately after the wedding. But the bride prevails on the Emperor to spare Juriste even though he has executed her brother. The Emperor consents and they live happily ever after.[5]

Muir mentions other sources in which the characters and actions resemble those in Cinthio's tale. Shakespeare, who wanted a happy ending, effected several changes to make the behavior of his characters less reprehensible. Angelo, though he breaks his promise to spare Claudio, does not succeed in having him executed; and Mariana is substituted for Isabella. Although these changes are melodramatic, they lend some plausibility to Isabella's actions. The fact that Claudio's crime is changed from rape to fornication with a girl he intends to marry makes his offense far less heinous and the proposed punishment extreme. Angelo's intentions may be as low as those of his prototypes, but he does not accomplish much evil; and Shakespeare is psychologically accurate enough in characterizing him to make his temptation understandable. For example, consider Angelo's soliloquy following his first interview with Isabella:

> What, do I love her,
> That I desire to hear her speak again?
> And feast upon her eyes? What is't I dream on?
> O cunning enemy, that, to catch a saint,
> With saints dost bait thy hook! . . .
>   Never could the strumpet,
> With all her double vigour—art and nature—
> Once stir my temper; but this virtuous maid
> Subdues me quite. Ever till now,
> When men were fond, I smil'd, and wond'red how.
>   (II:ii:177-187)

With the evidence of passages like this, I believe we must question the idea that Angelo is a hypocrite from the start, an outright villain like Iago and Richard III. Instead, we are faced with the problem of evaluating his effectiveness as a man tempted and fallen. Since *Measure for Measure* is a comedy in which everything comes out right for the good people, the effect of Angelo's villainy (as of Shylock's) is not fatal. Though for a time his intentions are as black as those of the blackest villains, the Duke, who is testing him, always controls the situation and protects innocent characters. Thus the play becomes not so much an imitation of life, in which no such benevolent and almost supernatural control could be expected, as an illustration of the theme: "with what measure ye mete, it shall be measured to you again." The thematic nature of the play is suggested by Angelo's words to Escalus, pleading for Claudio's life:

> You may not so extenuate his offence . . .
>   but rather tell me,
> When I that censure him do so offend,
> Let mine own judgment pattern out my death.
>   (II:i:27-30)

Angelo is here insisting on his brand of justice and the letter of the law; to his credit it should be added that, when his supposed

crimes are uncovered, he asks no less than death. He tells the
Duke,

> Then, good prince,
> No longer session hold upon my shame,
> But let my trial be mine own confession.
> Immediate sentence then, and sequent death,
> Is all the grace I beg.   (V:i:375-379)

And again:

> I am sorry that such sorrow I procure;
> And so deep sticks it in my penitent heart
> That I crave death more willingly than mercy.
> 'Tis my deserving, and I do entreat it.   (V:i:479-482)

In contrast to Angelo's strictness in dealing with Claudio (and
with himself when he is discovered in crime), is Isabella's Christian plea of tempering justice with mercy. The Christian note is
suggested early in the play in her reply to Angelo's statement that
her brother is "a forfeit of the law."

> Why, all the souls that were were forfeit once,
> And he that might the vantage best have took
> Found out the remedy. How would you be
> If he which is the top of judgment should
> But judge you as you are? O, think on that!
> And mercy then will breathe within your lips
> Like man new made.   (II:ii:73-79)

In the same scene she suggests that, were their roles reversed and
were Isabella to judge Angelo, she would show mercy:

> I would to heaven I had your potency
> And you were Isabel! Should it then be thus?
> No! I would tell what 'twere to be a judge,
> And what a prisoner.   (II:ii:67-70)

In the dénouement she is as good as her word and responds as
follows to Mariana's plea that Angelo's life be spared even while
Isabella is as yet unaware that her brother is alive:

> I partly think
> A due sincerity governed his deeds
> Till he did look on me. Since it is so,

Let him not die. My brother had but justice
In that he did the thing for which he died.
For Angelo,
His act did not o'ertake his bad intent,
And must be buried but as an intent
That perish'd by the way. Thoughts are no subjects,
Intents but merely thoughts.   (V:i:450-459)

Thus the cycle is complete, and harsh justice is tempered by Christian mercy. But what of the play? And especially what of the characterization of Angelo? We have J. I. M. Stewart's opinion (backed by a reference to Havelock Ellis) that

> just such men as Angelo, cold to common solicitations and believing themselves substantially insensible to sexual satis- factions . . . are liable to the kind of aberration depicted: sudden uncontrollable lust for a woman specially circum- stanced, or habited. This is certainly morbid; but psychology insists that responses like Angelo's shade into "normal" if irrational varieties of "love at first sight." [6]

Also, there is a degree of realism in the fact that one crime leads to another and that Angelo (like Macbeth) once he has embarked on crime—the clandestine meeting with the supposed Isabella— stops not at attempting murder because Claudio

> Might in the times to come have ta'en revenge
> By so receiving a dishonour'd life
> With ransom of such shame. Would yet he had liv'd!
> Alack, when once our grace we have forgot,
> Nothing goes right! we would, and we would not!
>   (IV:iv:32-36).

Although the play as a whole is not entirely satisfactory, the conflict between good and evil as represented by Isabella and Angelo develops in a way probably unique in Shakespeare's plays. In the first interview between Angelo and Isabella, she behaves illogically like a good woman who abhors the vice of which her brother stands convicted, but who can still pardon the offender in Christian fashion. Angelo is the cold and firm representative of justice who points out that offenders must be punished if the offense is to be stamped out, if innocent victims are to be protected, and if the criminal is to be prevented from repeating his crime. At the conclusion of this debate between the claims of mercy and justice, Angelo relents, at least to the extent of agreeing to see Isabella again.

During this first interview it is Isabella who puts into words the suggestion that, since they cannot reconcile their differences over the claims of justice and mercy, she must "bribe" him. She uses the term innocently enough and explains that her bribe will not be gold or jewels, but "true prayers." Perhaps this suggestion, together with her bearing and manner, leads Angelo to weaken in a way that neither of them would have supposed possible. As we have noted above, he admits to himself in soliloquy that he who has never before been tempted by illicit love is overcome by this virtuous woman. And just before she reappears in Scene iv, Angelo reveals that he, like Claudius, has tried to pray but can think of nothing except Isabella:

> When I would pray and think, I think and pray
> To several subjects. Heaven hath my empty words,
> Whilst my invention, hearing not my tongue,
> Anchors on Isabel. Heaven in my mouth,
> As if I did but only chew his name,
> And in my heart the strong and swelling evil
> Of my conception!   (II:iv:1-7)

Later in Scene iv Angelo mentions the way that Isabella can save Claudio; but the suggestion is made in such terms that, at first, Isabella thinks he is trying to drive home the fallacy of her point of view.

> ANGELO. . . . and that there were
> No earthly mean to save him but that either
> You must lay down the treasures of your body
> To this suppos'd, or else to let him suffer:
> What would you do? . . .
> ISABEL. Better it were a brother died at once
> Than that a sister, by redeeming him,
> Should die forever.
> ANGELO. Were not you then as cruel as the sentence
> That you have slander'd so?
> ISABEL. Ignomy in ransom and free pardon

Are of two houses. Lawful mercy
Is nothing kin to foul redemption.   (II:iv:94-113)

When Angelo expresses himself in unmistakable terms, she, for
the moment, proves her human frailty and does attempt bribery:

I will proclaim thee, Angelo, look for't.
Sign me a present pardon for my brother,
Or with an outstretch'd throat I'll tell the world aloud
What man thou art.   (II:iv:151-154)

But both Angelo and Isabella know that her threat cannot be
carried out because Isabella's accusation would never be believed.

In spite of these and other details of accurate characterization,
the overall impression of the play is unsatisfactory as drama because the play is too obviously designed to make the characters
subserve not only the plot, but the theme as well.

As with Angelo, critics divide sharply in their interpretation
of Shylock. There is little doubt that the Jew possesses vicious
traits; but the question as to whether he is more sinned against
than sinning frequently arises, and actors have played the role
of Shylock convincingly by interpreting him sympathetically or
by characterizing him as a grotesque, inhuman figure. If Shylock
represented absolute evil in conflict with good, he might more
easily be conceived of as a type villain. But some critics—and
these, I believe, overstate their case—regard the good and evil in
this play as about equally balanced. John Middleton Murry, for
example, says, "it would be a fine point in ethics to determine
whether [Antonio's] treatment of Shylock, or Shylock's treatment
of him, was the more inhuman." [7] The evidence for this statement seems to lie mainly in Antonio's reply to Shylock's accusation that Antonio has treated him meanly:

I am as like to call thee so again,
To spet on thee again, to spurn thee too.
If thou wilt lend this money, lend it not
As to thy friends—for when did friendship take
A breed for barren metal of his friend?
But lend it rather to thine enemy,

Who if he break, thou mayst with better face
Exact the penalty.   (I:iii:131-138)

This personal abuse of Shylock is, indeed, inexcusable; but there
is some evidence that the real basis of enmity between the two
grows out of Antonio's generosity toward his friends, a kindness
that interferes with Shylock's moneylending. Note Shylock's comment:

[aside] How like a fawning publican he looks!
I hate him for he is a Christian;
But more for that in low simplicity
He lends out money gratis and brings down
The rate of usance here with us in Venice.
If I can catch him once upon the hip,
I will feed fat the ancient grudge I bear him.
He hates our sacred nation, and he rails,
Even there where merchants most do congregate,
On me, my bargains, and my well-won thrift,
Which he calls interest. Cursed be my tribe
If I forgive him!   (I:iii:42-53)

Later when Antonio finds himself in the toils of the Jew, he explains,

I'll follow him no more with bootless prayers.
He seeks my life. His reason well I know:
I oft deliver'd from his forfeitures
Many that have at times made moan to me.
Therefore he hates me.   (III:iii:20-24)

This passage suggests that Shylock made a habit of squeezing
debtors and makes more plausible his subsequent fiendish behavior. Shylock himself seems to corroborate Antonio's accusation when he says, "I will have the heart of him if he forfeit;
for, were he out of Venice, I can make what merchandise I
will" (III:i:132-134).

Henry N. Hudson has made a fairer evaluation of the rela-
tionship between Antonio and Shylock. Hudson admits that Antonio's treatment of Shylock is a blemish on an otherwise generous character; but he adds that "the Jew, despite his provoca-
tions, avowedly grounds his hate mainly on those very things

which make the strongest title to a good man's love. For Shylock's revenge fastens not so much on [Antonio's] abuse of him as on his kindness to others." [8] Early in the play, before the full extent of Shylock's capacity for cruelty has been demonstrated, there is evidence that the Jew's personality is such as to alienate people who should show him love and respect. When Jessica learns that Launcelot Gobbo is leaving her father's service, she says,

> I am sorry thou wilt leave my father so.
> Our house is hell; and thou, a merry devil,
> Didst rob it of some taste of tediousness. (II:iii:1-3)

Jessica's unsatisfactory relations with her father bother her, as can be seen from her remarks at the close of Act II, Scene iii:

> Alack, what heinous sin is it in me
> To be asham'd to be my father's child!
> But though I am a daughter to his blood,
> I am not to his manners. O Lorenzo,
> If thou keep promise, I shall end this strife,
> Become a Christian and thy loving wife. (II:iii:16-21)

In view of the hostility that Shylock provokes in his own daughter and in the otherwise friendly Antonio, one might be surprised at the vehemence with which some critics take up Shylock's cause. To return to Murry,

> For in Shylock are combined, in a mighty imaginative creation, the passionate determination to revenge the secular wrongs of Jewry with a scorching and irrefutable indictment of the Christianity which inflicted them. He emerges in the play more as a Shakespearian hero than a Shakespearian villian. Compare him with Iago, and what has been called Iago's "motiveless malignity." The malignity of Shylock is more than motived; it is justified . . . If retribution be justice, Shylock's cause is just: and though his instinctive passion for revenge is indiscriminate in that it claims for victim a man who has done no worse—and no better—than despise and insult the Jew, we cannot condemn him . . . It is not until Shylock has deliberately refused Portia's great appeal for mercy that the issue turns against him.[9]

There is little in the text to substantiate such an interpretation of *The Merchant of Venice,* and one must conclude that critics who take this approach read the play as a chapter in the long and sometimes terrible persecution of the Jews.

There are, of course, those who take a less emotional view of the play. Historical critics who, like Stoll, insist that "a popular dramatist . . . even more than other artists, cannot play a lone hand, but must regard the established traditions of his art, the rooted sentiments and prejudices of his public," [10] have illuminated our understanding of the Jewish problem in Elizabethan England. Among other things, they have pointed out that the execution of Roderigo Lopez, the physician who was accused of plotting to poison the queen, became a cause célèbre in London and was widely discussed. It may be that Burbage, while playing Shylock, trimmed his beard to resemble Lopez' and that spectators witnessing the trial of Shylock in *The Merchant of Venice* were reminded of the trial of Lopez at which the Earl of Essex presided. In *Comic Characters of Shakespeare,* John Palmer notes that

> When Shakespeare sat down to write 'The Merchant of Venice' in 1594, anti-semitism was in fashion. Marlowe had exploited it four years previously . . . Barabbas, the Jew of Malta, embodied in his wicked person all the qualities which a persecuting majority commonly attributed to its victims. For four years Marlowe's Jew had held the stage and, during the excitement aroused by the trial of Lopez, between May and December, 1594, his play was twenty times revived.[11]

But none of these facts precludes the possibility of a sympathetic attitude toward the Jew existing in the minds of *some* people in Shakespeare's day (just as sympathy does exist in the minds of some people in our own or any other age). Palmer recognizes this possibility when he writes:

> The execution of Lopez, while it gratified the Jew-baiters, seems to have provoked indignation and even a searching of hearts among the more reasonable and sensitive citizens of London. Elizabeth, who believed that Lopez was innocent, at first refused to sign his death warrant. She yielded to pop-

ular clamour, stimulated by Essex and his friends, but against her better judgment. . . . even in Shakespeare's time opinions were divided on the Jewish question. . . . Shakespeare, in presenting Shylock to the public in 1594, was not writing for an audience incapable of appreciating the more humane aspects of his comedy.[12]

An opposite view of anti-Semitism in Shakespeare's England is expressed in an introduction to *The Merchant of Venice* by editors Wright and Freund:

> J. L. Cardozo in *The Contemporary Jew in the Elizabethan Drama* has given convincing proof that so few Jews were known in Shakespeare's England that he could not have been drawing Shylock's picture from any living prototype. To be sure, there was the case of the unfortunate Portuguese Jewish physician Dr. Roderigo Lopez, who was executed in June, 1594, for allegedly plotting against the life of Queen Elizabeth, but Lopez was a convert and if he suffered from prejudice at his trial it reflected the normal Elizabethan prejudice against foreigners, particularly Latins, and was not a result of his Jewish blood.[13]

So much for historical research. As for the conventions of the Elizabethan stage, we are reminded by Palmer that

> Marlowe's Barabbas still held the stage when Shakespeare created Shylock. The fashion was fixed and Shakespeare must seem to follow it. It did not matter how absurd or improbable the plot of his play might be, because the public was ready to believe anything about a Jew. Any horrible mischief which a Jew might contrive would be credited and any device by which the Jew might be foiled of his purpose, however childish or improbable, would be commended.[14]

Since Barabbas is Shylock's prototype, we should review his misdeeds before attempting to see what modifications Shakespeare made in creating his villain. To begin with, Barabbas seems badly used right at the beginning of the play. The governor of Malta insists that the rich Jews of the town give half of their estates as tribute to the Turks. When Barabbas refuses, the state confiscates his fortune. From then on, Barabbas engages in a series of crimes, some obviously retributive, others prompted either by his hatred of Christians or by his Machiavellian delight in double-dealing. He contrives that two Christian suitors for his daughter's hand, one of them the governor's son, should kill each other. Then when his daughter discovers this and goes to a nunnery, he poisons her together with all the nuns. He strangles a friar and poisons his servant. After delivering Malta to the Turks, he proposes to the captured governor of Malta that they conspire to destroy the Turks. This he partly succeeds in doing, but falls into a boiling cauldron that he had prepared for the Turkish leader. The whole play is so packed with sensational incident that there is no room for realistic characterization.

Although Shylock may have been conceived in the tradition of Marlowe's Barabbas, he emerges as something far more individualized. Marlowe's only advantage is in the original motivation. Barabbas is, as we have seen, badly used; and one's sympathy would go out to a victim of confiscatory taxation based on religious prejudice. Dramatically, this is a more clearly-defined motive than we have in *The Merchant of Venice*. Except for this initial advantage, however, Shakespeare has certainly improved on his prototype; and I am partly inclined to agree with Dowden's verdict that *"The Merchant of Venice* is probably the first of Shakespeare's comedies in which the study of character wholly dominates all other interests."* [15] In the poet's treatment of Shylock we probably come as close to psychological accuracy of characterization as in his delineation of any other villain thus far discussed. Shakespeare goes into some detail to explain the hatred existing between Shylock and Antonio:

> Signior Antonio, many a time and oft
> In the Rialto you have rated me
> About my moneys and my usances.
> Still have I borne it with a patient shrug;
> For suff'rance is the badge of all our tribe.
> You call me misbeliever, cutthroat dog,
> And spet upon my Jewish gaberdine,
> And all for use of that which is mine own.
> Well then, it now appears you need my help.
> Go to then, you come to me and you say,

'Shylock, we would have moneys.' You say so—
You that did void your rheum upon my beard
And foot me as you spurn a stranger cur
Over your threshold. Moneys is your suit.
What should I say to you? Should I not say
'Hath a dog money? Is it possible
A cur can lend three thousand ducats?' or
Shall I bend low, and in a bondman's key,
With bated breath and whisp'ring humbleness,
Say this:
'Fair sir, you spet on me on Wednesday last;
You spurn'd me such a day; another time
You call'd me dog; and for these courtesies
I'll lend you thus much moneys?'   (I:iii:107-130)

In his reply Antonio does not attempt to refute Shylock's charges; neither does he seek reconciliation. Up to this point we have open declarations of hatred; but, toward the end of Act I, Shylock, turning deceitful, feigns friendship and proposes the bond "in a merry sport" (I:iii:146). At least one critic believes that Shylock is sincere in thus proposing the bond. By carefully selecting passages from the text, H. B. Charlton argues that Shylock at first thought of charging interest, tried to justify the Hebrew custom of lending money at interest by reference to the *Old Testament* story of Jacob's thrift (I:iii:72-91), was moved by Antonio's remark, "When did friendship take/A breed for barren metal of his friend" (I:iii:134-135), and decides to be a friend of Antonio and Bassanio: "I would be friends with you and have your love" (I:iii:139). Although most critics regard this statement as evidence of Shylock's hypocrisy, Charlton thinks Shylock means what he says and that he was touched by Bassanio's remark, "This were kindness" (I:iii:144).

> And Shylock, jumping at this first expression of sympathy ever spoken to him, will settle the thing at once. Let them immediately devise a bond, and, remembering the general terms suggested previously by Antonio, but glossing them as if they could now be taken with friendly humour, let the bond include a forfeiture penalty, never likely, of course, to fall due, which will be a sort of extravagant parody of the contractual forfeits customary in bonds.[16]

If we are to believe Charlton's argument, it is only after Jessica's elopement that Shylock becomes distraught and seeks revenge. This interpretation does not, as I have said, square with the text; but we can agree with Charlton's conclusion that although the sources of Shakespeare's play included the forfeiture and the fiendish Jew, Shakespeare modifies the source to make the situation arise more naturally.

Throughout the play we see examples of Shylock's meanness and attempts at cruelty. Since his villainy is thwarted, he would make an excellent stock comic figure except that in the midst of our feeling of scorn and ridicule, we are moved to pity. After analyzing the play in detail, Palmer shows that Shylock is a comic character from beginning to end; yet he qualifies this conclusion as follows:

> But alas for logic and the categories! No-one can remain wholly insensible to the emotional impact of the play. The imaginative effort expended by Shakespeare in making his Jew a comprehensibly human figure has imparted to him a vitality that every now and then stifles laughter and freezes the smile on our lips. . . . Shakespeare took the comic Jew for a theme, and wrote . . . a comedy in which ridicule does not exclude compassion, in which sympathy and detachment are reconciled in the irony which is necessarily achieved by the comic spirit in a serene presentation of things as they are.[17]

Consider, for example, the scene in which Tubal plays upon Shylock's emotions, alternately feeding him information about his own losses and Antonio's distress. From one point of view, Shylock is nowhere more ridiculous, nor the situation more comical:

> SHYLOCK: Why, there, there, there, there! A diamond gone cost me two thousand ducats in Frankford! The curse never fell upon our nation till now; I never felt it till now. . . . I would my daughter were dead at my foot, and the jewels in her ear! . . .
> TUBAL: Yes, other men have ill luck too. Antonio, as I heard in Genoa—
> SHYLOCK: What, what, what? Ill luck, ill luck?

TUBAL: Hath an argosy cast away, coming from Tripolis.
SHYLOCK: I thank God! . . . Good news, good news! Ha, ha!
Where? in Genoa?
TUBAL: Your daughter spent in Genoa, as I heard, one night
fourscore ducats.   (III:i:87-114)

In such a scene laughter at the Jew's plight would surely pre-
dominate, unless it were stifled by a feeling of the meanness of
man. Yet earlier in this scene Shylock makes a pathetic speech,
one that reveals his predicament both as an individual and as a
member of an afflicted race:

SALERIO: Why, I am sure, if he forfeit, thou wilt not take his
flesh. What's that good for?
SHYLOCK: To bait fish withal. If it will feed nothing else, it
will feed my revenge. He hath disgrac'd me, and hind'red me
half a million; laugh'd at my losses, mock'd at my gains,
scorned my nation, thwarted my bargains, cooled my friends,
heated mine enemies—and what's his reason? I am a Jew.
Hath not a Jew eyes? Hath not a Jew hands, organs, dimen-
sions, senses, affections, passions? fed with the same food,
hurt with the same weapons, subject to the same diseases,
healed by the same means, warmed and cooled by the same
winter and summer as a Christian is? If you prick us, do we
not bleed? If you tickle us, do we not laugh? If you poison
us, do we not die? And if you wrong us, shall we not revenge?
If we are like you in the rest, we will resemble you in that.
If a Jew wrong a Christian, what is his humility? Revenge.
If a Christian wrong a Jew, what should his sufferance be by
Christian example? Why, revenge. The villany you teach
me I will execute, and it shall go hard but I will better the
instruction.   (III:i:53-76)

It is true that when this passage is cited as evidence of Shakespeare's sympathy for the Jews, the latter part, containing Shylock's remarks on revenge and villany taught him by Christians,
is usually omitted. And though the whole passage does *not* con-
tain the plea for tolerance often claimed for part of it, the pathos
of Shylock's predicament—and that of his race—is made evident.
The subsequent development of *The Merchant of Venice* is

familiar. Antonio's ventures supposedly miscarry, and Shylock insists that the law be fulfilled; when the merchant is about to expose his breast to the knife, a flaw in the Jew's prosecution is discovered. "This bond doth give thee here no jot of blood" (IV:i:305). Thus is Antonio saved and Shylock thwarted, and presumably one could leave the theatre with the feeling that justice had prevailed over evil. But is that the total effect of this play? Granted that we are glad to see the benevolent Antonio saved, does it follow that we can say about Shylock, "It serves him right"? By no means, for the characterization of Shylock is so thorough and so effective that he claims a disproportionate share of our interest and, to some spectators, a large measure of sympathy.

These facts are mentioned to show that Shylock becomes more than an obstacle in Antonio's journey toward happiness and prosperity, which is about all one expects of a villain in the conventional comedy involving a young and promising hero who is destined to success in spite of the stumbling blocks the author places in his path. It is not because Shylock's intentions are less wicked than those of other villains that he appears more like a human being and less like a character whose course of action is limited and confined by the demands of plot. It is rather because Shakespeare took such pains to explain why Shylock acted as he did. Shylock's position is an understandable one; his reasons for desiring revenge are those with which we can sympathize. Add to this the fact that Shylock represents the underdog, and the emotional basis for conceiving of him as an object of pity is complete. Throughout the play he stands in lonely isolation, separated from Antonio and his host of friends. The treatment of Shylock during the latter part of the trial scene is pathetic. Gratiano turns Shylock's own remarks about "A Daniel come to judgment" (IV,i,223) back upon him. Though this scene has obvious comic elements, the measure for measure dealt to Shylock is such that only those who delight in cruelty and revenge could relish it. Not only is he made to give up most of his wealth, but also is he forced to become a Christian; these two demands seem so unbearable as to call forth his last pathetic utterance:

Nay, take my life and all! Pardon not that!
You take my house when you do take the prop
That doth sustain my house. You take my life
When you do take the means whereby I live.
    (IV:i:374-377)

Considered by himself, Shylock has appealed to many as one of the finest examples of psychologically accurate characterization that Shakespeare ever achieved; but if we consider him in relation to his play, we may conclude that the human quality of the Jew is overdrawn. Early in this book I stated that lifelike characterization tends to increase the effectiveness of a drama, but one should realize that there is a point beyond which intricate and detailed characterization may become a detriment. For example, in a play where emphasis is usually divided between action and character, we obviously could not have as much detailed characterization as in a novel without slowing down the performance. In *The Merchant of Venice* we discover another problem, that of a villain characterized so thoroughly that the audience sympathizes with him and cannot feel that his punishment represents the triumph of justice over evil. Thus the effect of the play is distorted until it becomes different from what one would ordinarily expect of a comedy. Shylock, technically the antagonist, looms disproportionately large and actually becomes the leading figure; whereas Antonio is relegated to a lesser role. I believe, therefore, that although Shylock is admirably drawn, he is over-characterized for the role he was supposed to play.

V. REGAN, GONERIL, EDMUND, AND CLAUDIUS

Regan, Goneril, Edmund, and Claudius do not dominate their plays to the same extent as do the villains already discussed. Obviously, Lear and Hamlet are the chief characters in their plays; yet the characterization of the villains in these plays has, I believe, a bearing on the success of these two tragedies. Earlier I quoted Lamb as saying that "the plays of Shakespeare are less calculated for performance on a stage, than those of almost any other dramatist whatever." [1] Clearly this generalization is not true, as witness the stage history of some of Shakespeare's most successful plays, but I think Lamb's statement that "the Lear of Shakespeare cannot be acted," comes closer to the truth. The stage history of *Lear* is meagre compared with that of the other three great tragedies. One of the many problems of presenting *Lear* successfully is the unconvincing motivation at the beginning of the play, particularly the behavior of Lear and his daughters. Many critics have tried to explain the opening scenes.

Coleridge, for example, describes the division of the kingdom, something that apparently has been decided upon when the play opens, as intended to reveal those aspects of Lear's character on which the tragedy depends. That Lear is in his dotage seems obvious, but Coleridge's observation is more complex. According to him, the division scene depicts Lear as a man characterized by an "intense desire to be intensely beloved, selfish, and yet characteristic of the selfishness of a loving and kindly nature." [2]

Yet one can search through the early scenes of the play without finding much evidence in the king of this loving and kindly nature, except for his initial, ill-advised act of generosity in dividing his kingdom among his daughters. Much has been written about the inhumanity of Lear's older daughters and about the tactlessness of Cordelia; but what one sees first is Lear's inhumanity toward Cordelia, Kent, and Goneril. It may be that Shakespeare first shows us the violence of Lear not only to indicate that he is in his dotage and to reveal those aspects of his character on which the tragedy is to depend, but also to provide some motivation and some degree of plausibility for the villainy of Regan and Goneril. We have already noted that, whenever effective motivation of villains is found, it is most likely to appear in the early, expository scenes.

Although, as I shall try to show, the motivation of Regan and Goneril is not so clearly set forth as that of Edmund, significant clues for their behavior are not lacking in the opening scenes. For example, Lear says of Cordelia, 'I lov'd her most" (I:i:125), a statement corroborated by Goneril's remark, "He always lov'd our sister most" (I:i:293). Both these statements suggest that Regan and Goneril have faced a problem common enough in real life, that of a parent favoring one of his children over the others. Also, if we believe Lear's two older daughters, the example of his towering rage toward Cordelia and Kent with which the play opens is something that the girls have suffered under before. Goneril says, "The best and soundest of his time hath been but rash" (I:i:298). Anticipating the difficulties they may expect from their father during his monthly visits, Regan replies, "Such unconstant starts are we like to have from him as this of Kent's banishment" (I:i:304-305). Lear is not long in demonstrating what his daughters mean. When Goneril suggests that the king reduce his retinue of a hundred knights, he calls her "Degenerate bastard!" and "Detested kite" (I:iv:275,284)! In fact, the fidelity of good people like Kent and Cordelia to this irascible man is perhaps more difficult to account for than the first relatively mild examples of Regan's and Goneril's ingratitude.

Probably the elder daughters' capacity for villainy is suspected from the start, not by Lear, but by Cordelia. Before the two elder sisters have done anything blameworthy in the play—if we except their false declarations of love to their father—Cordelia suggests that she knows them for what they are. As she leaves with France, she says:

> I know you what you are;
> And, like a sister, am most loath to call
> Your faults as thy are nam'd. Use well our father.
> To your professed bosoms I commit him;

But yet, alas, stood I within his grace,
I would prefer him to a better place.   (I:i:272-277)

It must be admitted that Regan and Goneril are quick to live up to their reputation. Their conspiracy to break their part of the agreement with Lear, which was to provide shelter for their father and his knights, each for a month at a time, proceeds with ruthless speed. In the fourth scene of Act II, Lear utters one of his first pathetic remarks after trying to arouse the sympathy of Regan over Goneril's ungracious behavior: "I gave you all" (II:iv:252). Soon after this, he goes out into the storm.

So far we have considered Regan and Goneril as a pair, as if they had no separate identity. In fact, however, they are differentiated although I suspect that many a Shakespearean scholar would be hard put to explain the difference between the two evil sisters if the question were raised suddenly. Agnes Mure Mackenzie, in *The Women in Shakespeare's Plays,* believes that Goneril is the more self-possessed and the craftier, while Regan is more emotional and takes great delight in physical cruelty. According to Mackenzie, "there is a sort of heavy-handed compellingness about [Goneril] always, of a person absolutely sure both of her rightness and her power." [3] In her arguments with Lear about the misbehavior of his servants and the folly of his maintaining so large a retinue, "she begins, as she always does, by putting her opponent thoroughly and expeditiously in the wrong, and then telling him his scolding is for his own good." [4] What a lifelike quality this is, and how often have we all observed it, though fortunately not in people possessed of Goneril's fiendish qualities.

What we can never forget about Regan is her sadistic delight in torturing Gloucester. Goneril, Edmund, and Oswald leave just as Gloucester is brought in and tied to a chair. Note Regan's part in this horrible scene.

CORNWALL: Bind him, I say. [Servants bind him.]
REGAN: Hard, hard. O filthy traitor!
GLOUCESTER: Unmerciful lady as you are, I am none.
CORNWALL: To this chair bind him . . . [Regan plucks his beard]   (III:vii:31-34)

After Cornwall has plucked out one of Gloucester's eyes, Regan says, "One side will mock another. Th'other too" (III:vii:71)! When Cornwall's servant implores his lord to stop, Regan "takes a sword and runs at him behind." As if her inciting Cornwall to further torture of the old man and to participate in the fight were not enough, Regan caps her heinous deeds with verbal taunting of the helpless, blinded Gloucester.

> GLOUCESTER: All dark and comfortless! Where's my son Edmund?
> Edmund, enkindle all the sparks of nature
> To quit this horrid act.
> REGAN: Out, treacherous villain!
> Thou call'st on him that hates thee. It was he
> That made the overture of thy treasons to us;
> Who is too good to pity thee. . . .
> REGAN: Go thrust him out at gates, and let him smell
> His way to Dover.   (III:vii:85-93)

Although this is the most terrible example of Regan's cruelty, it is not unique. Earlier in the play Cornwall puts Kent in the stocks.

> CORNWALL: Fetch forth the stocks! As I have life and honour,
> There shall he sit till noon.
> REGAN: Till noon? Till night, my lord, and all night too!
>   (II:ii:140-142)

Small wonder that Mackenzie concludes her comments on this villain with the remark, "Leaving out Pandarus and Thersites, [Regan] is probably the most horrible figure Shakespeare ever created—certainly one of the very few for whom one feels a quite unmitigated loathing." [5]

Mackenzie pays a profound tribute to Shakespeare's powers of characterization when she observes, not only the differences between the two older sisters, but also—and this is ironic—the fact that the two villains are plainly kin to Cordelia.

> All three of the women are characters simple enough. The subtlety of their drawing is not in any of them singly, but rather in the way in which they are handled as a group. For they are sisters: conspicuously, indubitably kin to each

other and to their common father. They inherit much from him, indeed. All have his self-assertiveness and his hot blood. Goneril and Cordelia have far more strength than he has, largely because they are narrow in vision: they can only see a thing from their own point of view. It is this, indeed, that gives Goneril her deadly power: she is completely sure of herself. It is the same thing, applied with absolute honesty and even unselfishness, that makes Cordelia ruin both herself and Lear. For in the long run, though the evil is Goneril's, the *blame* is fundamentally Cordelia's and Lear's.[6]

I think many critics would agree with Mackenzie's attributing the responsibility for the tragedy to Lear and Cordelia, but I do not believe that Goneril "is invariably sure of her own righteousness —or if not, can soon enough convince herself." [7] She may start, as in the arguments with Lear over his servants, by blaming her opponent. But this is strategy that need not be sincere.

In the fourth act we see that Regan and Goneril have added lust for Edmund to their other crimes. Goneril plans to murder her husband, Albany, so that she, as a widow, can have Edmund. When she learns that Regan's husband, Cornwall, is dead, she becomes jealous of her sister who, as a widow, thinks she has a prior claim on Edmund's affections. This rivalry between the sisters brings about their downfall. In Act V Goneril poisons Regan and then stabs herself.

In contrast to the behavior of Regan and Goneril, the villainy of Edmund is somewhat more convincingly motivated. To begin with, his rivalry with his father and brother, though villainous, is more readily understandable than Regan and Goneril's treatment of Lear. To the typical audience, I suppose, none of the family ties are ordinarily thought to be closer and freer from rivalry than those which bind a father and his daughters. A son may contend for his father's or his brother's place, as Edmund does. Edmund is also, in some respects, a type villain. The fact that he is a bastard son would tend to make Elizabethan audiences accept his misconduct without question. But he is more than a type. He is given a past that, besides producing the effect of continuity in his character, also provides a partially satisfactory motive for the brutal action in which he engages.

Consequently, his actions become understandable in terms of human motivation instead of being conceived of as merely fulfilling demands of plot. Consider the following dialogue, spoken in Edmund's presence, with which the play opens:

> KENT: Is not this your son, my lord?
>
> GLOUCESTER: His breeding, sir, hath been at my charge. I have so often blush'd to acknowledge him that now I am braz'd to't.
>
> KENT: I cannot conceive you.
>
> GLOUCESTER: Sir, this young fellow's mother could; whereupon she grew round-womb'd, and had indeed, sir, a son for her cradle ere she had a husband for her bed. Do you smell a fault?
>
> KENT: I cannot wish the fault undone, the issue of it being so proper.
>
> GLOUCESTER: But I have, sir, a son by order of law, some year elder than this, who yet is no dearer in my account. Though this knave came something saucily into the world before he was sent for, yet was his mother fair, there was good sport at his making, and the whoreson must be acknowledged. (I:i:8-24)

Although this passage may have been written partly to amuse the audience, it also provides exposition. Gloucester takes little pains to conceal the fact of Edmund's bastardy. He also states that Edmund's bastardy has been a source of embarrassment to the father. We may infer that the illegitimate son has suffered mental anguish from the realization and reminder of his status. According to Coleridge, Edmund

> hears his mother and the circumstances of his birth spoken of with a most degrading and licentious levity. . . . This, and the consciousness of its notoriety . . . is the ever-trickling flow of wormwood and gall into the wounds of pride, the corrosive virus which inoculates pride with a venom not its own, with . . . pangs of shame personally undeserved and therefore felt as wrongs, and a blind ferment of vindictive workings towards the occasions and causes, especially towards a brother whose stainless birth and lawful honors were the constant remembrancers of *his* debasement.[8]

It is little to the purpose that Kittredge chides Coleridge for not perceiving "that 11. 1-24 are spoken in a private conversation between Kent and Gloucester, and that Edmund stands in the background and hears nothing until he is called forward ('Do you know this noble gentleman, Edmund?') to be introduced to 'my Lord of Kent' " [9] Although Kittredge's interpretation of the stage business is ingenious, what the audience sees is Kent, Gloucester, *and Edmund* together in the first scene. Even if Edmund does stand back during the first part of the conversation, not to come forward until line 25, as the stage directions in Kittredge's text read, the audience sees the three men together; and if there is any doubt in the audience's mind as to whether the conversation between Kent and Gloucester is supposed to be representative of what Edmund hears or overhears about his plight, that doubt is resolved by Edmund's soliloquy in the next scene:

> Thou, Nature, art my goddess; to thy law
> My services are bound. Wherefore should I
> Stand in the plague of custom, and permit
> The curiosity of nations to deprive me,
> For that I am some twelve or fourteen moonshines
> Lag of a brother? Why bastard? wherefore base?
> When my dimensions are as well compact,
> My mind as generous, and my shape as true,
> As honest madam's issue? Why brand they us
> With base? with baseness? bastardy? base, base?
> Who, in the lusty stealth of nature, take
> More composition and fierce quality
> Than doth, within a dull, stale, tired bed,
> Go to th'creating a whole tribe of fops
> Got 'tween asleep and wake?   (I:ii:1-15)

In this passage we see Edmund's mind at work: we see him brooding over his unfortunate plight, we hear him ask why he is stigmatized for something which he rightly regards as no fault of his. Edmund uses his unfortunate predicament as an excuse for villainy. Since he is a product of unconventional conduct, he decides to flout moral considerations. Although this shows a perversion in character, it is certainly understandable. Nor is it difficult to imagine the jealousy that Edmund feels toward Edgar, who is destined to inherit all their father's possessions. Edmund also has some traces of the liveliness that characterizes villains like Richard III and Iago. In his wit and vivaciousness we see how the effect of realistic characterization can be achieved by having a character talk in a way that amuses his audience and impresses them with his liveliness. After Edmund has forged the letter by which he plans to set his father against Edgar, he talks with his brother and apprises him of the danger confronting him. On this occasion he toys with Edgar and uses dramatic irony.

> EDGAR: Some villain hath done me wrong.
> EDMUND: That's my fear. I pray you have a continent for-bearance till the speed of his rage goes slower; and, as I say, retire with me to my lodging, from whence I will fitly bring you to hear my lord speak. Pray ye, go! There's my key. If you do stir abroad, go arm'd.
> EDGAR: Arm'd brother?
> EDMUND: Brother, I advise you to the best. Go arm'd. I am no honest man if there be any good meaning toward you. I have told you what I have seen and heard; but faintly, nothing like the image and horror of it. Pray you, away!
> (I:ii:180-192)

Scenes like this add the dimension of wit and irony to what might otherwise have been a flat villain like Aaron.

There is, however, at least one aspect of Edmund's characterization which, in my opinion, detracts from his effectiveness. After following evil throughout the play, he is suddenly moved by Edgar's speech describing the death of Gloucester and attempts to do some good before he dies. He tries to get through a reprieve for Lear and Cordelia, whom he has condemned to death.

> I pant for life. Some good I mean to do,
> Despite of mine own nature. Quickly send
> (Be brief in't) to the castle; for my writ
> Is on the life of Lear and on Cordelia.
> Nay, send in time.   (V:iii:243-247)

Although one might argue that inconsistency is a human quality and that repentance is characteristic of the dying, Edmund's last words provide a clear example of a character's subservience to plot, for he is the only one who knows about the plight of Lear and Cordelia. Just before this passage, Edmund makes another statement that reveals a pathetic, human quality in this social outcast. When the bodies of Goneril and Regan are brought in, Edmund says:

> Yet Edmund was belov'd.
> The one the other poisoned for my sake,
> And after slew herself.   (V:iii:239-241)

This, too, is expository, a tying up of the loose ends of plot; it also adds an unexpected bit of characterization in which Edmund reveals the universal quality of needing to be loved, if only by creatures like Regan and Goneril.

Of the three villains in *Lear,* Edmund seems to be the most nearly lifelike even though, as we have observed, there is at least one serious flaw in his characterization. Also, the fact that, at the beginning of the play he functions in a subplot paralleling the main theme of filial ingratitude might raise questions of plausibility. I think Shakespeare's device of having the subplot follow the main plot so closely creates an atmosphere of unreality; it is as if he were striving too obviously to emphasize a theme. This may be good poetry, but bad theatre. Even more serious a fault, in my opinion, is making Edmund a more convincing villain than either Regan or Goneril. The play might be more effective on the stage if the *chief* villains, Regan and Goneril, who are concerned with the main plot from the beginning, had been more realistically characterized.

I have said that Claudius belongs to that class of villains who do not dominate their plays to the same extent as do those discussed earlier. He could be contrasted with Iago in several ways: It is obvious that Iago dominates his play; in fact, he is given a few more lines than Othello. It is equally obvious that all the other characters in *Hamlet* play relatively minor roles when compared with the protagonist; and students of Shakespeare might find it difficult to guess the relative importance, measured by length of speaking parts, of the other characters. Actually Claudius has the second longest part, though he is given only one-third as many lines as Hamlet.

Another significant difference between Claudius and Iago is the time when their crimes take place. When *Othello* opens, Iago's crimes are all ahead of him; heretofore one may assume that he has served Othello well enough to be held in high esteem; and the chief cause for Iago's hatred of his general, as explained in the opening scene of the play, is of recent origin. But with Claudius the situation is different. When the curtain rises in *Hamlet,* Claudius has already committed the most heinous of crimes; fratricide, regicide, incest, adultery. Yet I think those critics err who find too great a discrepancy between Claudius' past behavior and his conduct during the second scene of Act I when he makes his first appearance in the play. Hamlet tells us "That one may smile, and smile, and be a villain" (I:v:108); we scarcely need this reminder that hypocrisy and dissimulation are lifelike qualities.

In fact, it seems to me that one of the most convincing features of Claudius' characterization is his hypocrisy, which merits comparison with that of Richard III and Iago. Both of the latter are probably more interesting villains than Claudius because of their greater liveliness and because they dominate their plays to a much greater degree than does Claudius; but for hypocrisy alone, Claudius probably outdistances even these two formidable rivals. The hypocrisy of Richard III is melodramatic. Even without his own declaration of allegiance to evil, no one in the audience would be likely to conceive of Shakespeare's Richard as anything but an out-and-out villain. But let us examine the second scene of the first act of *Hamlet,* where Claudius first appears.

Assuming that we know nothing about his character—and nothing has been revealed in the opening scene of the play—the king strikes us as a dignified, kindly, efficient ruler: he speaks with love and respect of his deceased brother and of his new queen, he handles state affairs with efficiency and dispatch, he graciously grants Laertes permission to return to Paris. Even later in the scene when he reproves Hamlet for persevering "in obstinate condolement," calling that attitude "a course/Of impious stubbornness" (I:ii:93-4), the king is, if not tactful, at least—on the surface—well-meaning. Nor can the audience—and I mean an audience unfamiliar with the play—be expected to share immediately Hamlet's feeling when the king tells him— him whose place on the throne Claudius has usurped through murder and incest—that he loves him like a son:

> think of us
> As of a father; for let the world take note
> You are the most immediate to our throne,
> And with no less nobility of love
> Than that which dearest father bears his son
> Do I impart toward you.   (I:ii:107-112)

Unless we accept Howard Mumford Jones's interpretation, which will be explained later, this is, of course, the speech of a rank hypocrite. But at this stage of the play even Hamlet does not know that his uncle murdered his father. It is not until later in the scene, when Hamlet hears Horatio's account of the appearance of his father's ghost, that Hamlet first suspects foul play. Whether or not Hamlet is concerned about his place on the throne having been usurped is a matter for conjecture. All that Hamlet tells us this early in the play is that he is deeply distressed by his mother's hasty remarriage and that he dislikes his uncle, whom he compares unfavorably with his father.

Of course, if Claudius is portrayed as a melodramatic stage villain, and if his lines are spoken in an obviously hypocritical manner, his true nature becomes at once apparent; but there is certainly material in this scene for a true-to-life revelation of man's capacity for duplicity, for living and acting a lie. In fact, Bertram Joseph finds a special, ironic quality in Claudius' hypocrisy. In *Conscience and the King*, he writes:

> The peculiar quality of this hypocrite lies in his ability **not** merely to hide evil, but to present it openly when he chooses, in a manner which leads ordinary people not to recognize it emotionally for what it is, but to respond to it as good. Claudius reminds his listeners that his behaviour

could indeed be regarded as not in accordance with what is normally held as the best of taste:

Though yet of Hamlet our dear brother's death
The memory be green, and that it us befitted
To bear our hearts in grief, and our whole kingdom
To be contracted in one brow of woe,
Yet so far hath discretion fought with nature
That we with wisest sorrow think on him
Together with remembrance of ourselves.

As this scene develops, with an obviously admiring court and a loving queen, from none of whom comes any hint of shame or disapproval, it is easy to accept Claudius' words as perfectly reasonable, and to forget that he is guilty of at the least a gross breach of etiquette in marrying so soon and in putting an end to court mourning within two months of the last king's death. . . . he has managed to marry his brother's widow without stimulating in his courtiers their normal reaction to incest; and yet in this case, too, he does not attempt to hide what he has done; he merely contrives to make the world mistake the real quality of his actions:

Therefore, our sometime sister, now our queen, . . .
Have we, as 'twere with a defeated joy, . . .
Taken to wife; nor have we herein barr'd
Your better wisdoms, which have freely gone
With this affair along.

It is the measure of his uncle's success that Hamlet, the only person to react normally to an abnormal situation, is himself made to seem abnormal.[10]

But some critics, Levin Schücking, for example, believe that the characterization of Claudius violates a principle of the drama, "namely, that the action must not be dependent on qualities which are not shown by the respective persons in the course of the drama." Schücking applies this principle to Claudius and finds a problem in his characterization:

A dreadful crime has been committed, presupposing a character such as can be found only among the outcasts of humanity. A trustful, unsuspecting brother has been assassinated; the man who has blackened his soul with this enormous guilt must manifest a nature to correspond with it. We expect his malevolence and baseness to appear in his character. The qualities which make him a murderer should come out clearly in his relation to his environment even after he has attained his object.[11]

Such a remark seems to overlook completely the varying temperaments that probably exist among murderers. Even though a man like Macbeth may become unnerved after committing murder and almost reveal his guilt in public as in the banquet scene, villains like Claudius seem on their first appearance to be able to bear the burden of capital crime with scarcely a shudder.

And even if one had no reason to demur from Schücking's theory of character representation, I do not see that it applies to Claudius. What troubles Schücking, apparently, is that Claudius' true nature is not revealed *immediately* on his first appearance. But such a characterization would reduce the king to a type villain. All that Schücking's own rule requires is that character should be revealed *in the course of* the drama, not necessarily at its beginning. And our discovery, bit by bit, of the blackness of Claudius is, in my opinion, much more lifelike than what Schücking seems to propose. We are not left long in doubt about Claudius: Hamlet characterizes him unfavorably and the ghost accuses him of murder, incest, and adultery:

> GHOST: . . . But know, thou noble youth,
> The serpent that did sting thy father's life
> Now wears his crown.
> HAMLET: O my prophetic soul!
> My uncle?
> GHOST: Ay, that incestuous, that adulterate beast,
> With witchcraft of his wit, with traitorous gifts—
> O wicked wit and gifts, that have the power
> So to seduce!—won to his shameful lust
> The will of my most seeming-virtuous queen.   (I:v:38-46)

And if the characterization of the king by his nephew and the ghost were not sufficiently plain, Claudius' self-accusation in the moments when his conscience troubles him adds the final touch.

I think that Claudius' conscience is nearly as convincing a character trait as his hypocrisy. An examination of Claudius' remorse
will show that this trait is realistically portrayed. It is clearly
not the kind of remorse that we find in Edmund, remorse introduced for no other purpose than to advance the plot.

With Claudius, remorse occurs as occasions in the play re-
mind him of the blackness of his villainy. Claudius' thinking is
represented as something more than a means for explaining certain elements of the plot to the audience. It is not true, as
Schücking maintains, "that the action could not dispense with
the prayer scene, inasmuch as it is the only means of giving the
spectator the final confirmation, which is urgently required, that
the events related by the ghost have actually taken place in the
manner described." [12] The prayer scene may provide final confirmation; but after the play within a play, the audience has no
more reason to doubt Claudius' guilt than Hamlet has. Claudius'
aside and his prayer in Act III are examples of self-revelation;
for Claudius faces questions that probably confront every sane
criminal at one time or another, namely, the possibility of repentance and reform, and the inevitability of a day of reckon-
ing either in this world or in the next. Claudius is well aware
of his sins; Polonius unintentionally reminds him of them in
Act III, Scene i:

> Ophelia, walk you here.—Gracious, so please you,
> We will bestow ourselves.—[*To Ophelia*] Read on this
>   book,
> That show of such an exercise may colour
> Your loneliness.—We are oft to blame in this,
> 'Tis too much prov'd, that with devotion's visage
> And pious action we do sugar o'er
> The devil himself.
> KING:[aside] O, 'tis too true!
> How smart a lash that speech doth give my conscience!
> The harlot's cheek, beautied with plast'ring art,
> Is not more ugly to the thing that helps it
> Than is my deed to my most painted word.
> O heavy burthen!   (III:i:43-54)

And in Act III, Scene iii, Claudius soliloquizes:

O, my offence is rank, it smells to heaven;
It hath the primal eldest curse upon't,
A brother's murther! Pray can I not,
Though inclination be as sharp as will.
My stronger guilt defeats my strong intent;
And, like a man to double business bound,
I stand in pause where I shall first begin,
And both neglect. What if this cursed hand
Were thicker than itself with brother's blood,
Is there not rain enough in the sweet heavens
To wash it white as snow? Whereto serves mercy
But to confront the visage of offence?
And what's in prayer but this two-fold force,
To be forestalled ere we come to fall,
Or pardon'd, being down? Then I'll look up;
My fault is past. But, O, what form of prayer
Can serve my turn? 'Forgive me my foul murther'?
That cannot be; since I am still possess'd
Of those effects for which I did the murther—
My crown, mine own ambition, and my queen.
May one be pardon'd and retain the offence?
In the corrupted currents of this world
Offence's gilded hand may shove by justice,
And oft 'tis seen the wicked prize itself
Buys out the law; but 'tis not so above.
There is no shuffling; there the action lies
In his true nature, and we ourselves compell'd,
Even to the teeth and forehead of our faults,
To give in evidence. What then? What rests?
Try what repentance can. What can it not?
Yet what can it when one cannot repent?
O wretched state! O bosom black as death!
O limed soul, that, struggling to be free,
Art more engag'd! Help, angels! Make assay.
Bow, stubborn knees; and heart with strings of steel,
Be soft as sinews of the new-born babe.
All may be well.   (III:iii:36-72)

Ruth Anderson comments intelligently on Claudius' plight in her *Elizabethan Psychology and Shakespeare's Plays:* "Claudius . . . possesses some trace of conscience, and he actually tries to pray. In such cases he sees his crime as 'unlawful and unbecoming.' He sees it usually, however, 'drest up in all its gay Attire, with all the Circumstances of Pleasure and Profit'—his crown, his own ambition, and his queen. He is wise enough to know that he cannot be pardoned and retain the effects." [13]

This hopeless dilemma in which Claudius is placed, this difficulty of not being able to repent of his murder or to receive pardon for it because he is "still possessed of those effects for which [he] did the murther," seems to be a realistic and understandable human problem. For, although most of us are not guilty of a sin which has "the primal eldest curse upon't," many of us do commit faults about which our consciences work in a pattern similar to Claudius'; and when we see in the workings of a character's mind a reasoning process similar to one that we have used, that character becomes for us more realistic and more nearly human; we tend to regard him as an individual with problems of his own rather than as one of several interdependent parts of a complex drama. Claudius stimulates that interest and succeeds in claiming our understanding, if not our sympathy, because Shakespeare has made effective use of an important element in realistic characterization, the element of identity between spectator and character.

Some critics even find grounds on which to sympathize with Claudius and to praise him for the love and consideration he shows Gertrude and for the way in which he conducts affairs of state in Denmark. In *The Heart of Hamlet*, Bernard Grebanier finds Claudius' love for his queen a mitigating feature in his character:

> There is a part of [Claudius'] life which partakes of nobility, and that is his love for his wife. It is very plain that he wished to marry Gertrude not for the crown alone but because of his love for her. He says as much to God, when he is baring his soul and its motives. . . . when the younger man [Laertes] asks him why, if Hamlet, as Claudius has said, "pursued" the king's life, Claudius took no measures against his stepson:
>
> > The Queen his mother
> > Lives almost by his looks; and for myself,—

My virtue or my plague, be it either which,—
She's so conjunctive to my life and soul
That, as the star moves not but in his sphere,
I could not but by her. . . .

Not once during the entire course of the drama does Claudius ever say a disparaging thing concerning Hamlet to the
Queen. . . . Hamlet in their presence is untiring in his insults to the King; Claudius may bite his lip, but his answer
to the Prince is always polite. . . . A clever man, his motives, as with all of us, are mixed; his forbearance with
Hamlet—publicly—can only redound to his credit and
Hamlet's obloquy. But there is no doubt that his forced
patience is also born of his desire to spare the Queen any
hurt. . . . Claudius's considerateness of Gertrude is the one
truly elevated aspect of his character. He has spared her all
participation in, all knowledge of her first husband's murder, and he continues sparing her by suppressing his growing hatred of Hamlet so that she need not be torn between
her love for both of them. He definitely limits his own
freedom of action against the Prince, through his protective-
ness of his wife, and for her sake bears the brunt of Hamlet's public derision—a difficult task for a man of his strong
character.[14]

The chief flaw in Grebanier's argument, as I see it, is that sparing Gertrude the knowledge of how her first husband met his
death may be more than a tender consideration for her feelings. Claudius may have deceived her to accomplish his ends.
Of course, we do not know whether Gertrude would have been
a willing accomplice in the murder or whether she would have
married Claudius had she known what he had done. Critics
have tried to build a case for Gertrude's complete innocence of
the murder and for her partial or full implication in it, but it
is certainly begging the question to assume that Claudius' motive
was entirely selfless. Still his apparent love and tenderness for
Gertrude cannot be overlooked in evaluating his character;
Shakespeare has made something of it although Grebanier may
be overstating the case.

There is another positive aspect of Claudius' character which
many critics have noticed though none have defended it so

strongly as did Howard Mumford Jones in "The King in Hamlet." The essence of Jones's thesis is that Claudius, though guilty
of a terrible crime, is no mere villain. Jones seems to read the play
as a chapter in the troubled history of Denmark and concludes
that the old Hamlet would have ruined his country had he lived
on, that young Hamlet is obviously unsuited for a statesman's
role, and that Claudius is just such a ruler as Denmark needs
and deserves. Some of Jones's comments, though extreme, reveal
how even the blackest villains, in drama as in real life, may
claim their supporters.

> Why, then, did [Claudius] kill his brother? . . . why did he
> desire to become king? . . . Was it not . . . the itch of com-
> petency to seize the office in which Claudius felt his extraor-
> dinary powers would have their widest play? . . . And so,
> combining desire and policy, Claudius seduces Gertrude
> and murders Hamlet. Having seduced the queen he comes,
> in his fashion, to love her. Having murdered his brother,
> he comes to repent. . . . He comes to the throne amid general
> approbation, and promptly and skillfully seizes the reins
> of government. There is no move which a wise ruler should
> make that he does not make. . . . No one knows of his crime.
> He resolves to do penance for it by a life devoted to wise
> and good actions.

> The King does his best; he is extremely patient with his
> nephew; and it is only when his own royal life is in danger,
> as the play scene and the death of Polonius tell him, that
> . . . he reluctantly decides to sacrifice Hamlet. . . . It is, if
> you will, a selfish performance, and Claudius' motives, like
> all human motives, are mixed, but his action is a consid-
> ered one, and in view of Hamlet's lack of capacity for gov-
> ernment, may well be for the good of Denmark.

> [Claudius] has labored for the good of Denmark, . . . has
> staved off Norway, exhausted diplomacy to avoid an im-
> broglio with Poland and young Fortinbras.

> [old Hamlet is] a hero king, but a king, it is perfectly ob-
> vious, who, if he continues, will ruin Denmark which he
> regards, indeed, as so much personal property. Add that
> human lives mean as little to him as they did to Napoleon.[15]

All this speculation as to the course of Danish history under the Hamlets or Claudius is undertaken to show that Claudius is not merely a stage villain, as Jones claims he is usually played, but a complex personality of mixed motives. His essay is an attempt to correct the balance which always makes so much of Hamlet to the detriment of all other characters in the play. Jones is probably correct in stating that Claudius is usually played as a serious and heavy character in contrast to Hamlet, who is lively and versatile.

Because Claudius does not dominate his play to the same extent that most of the other villains we have discussed dominate theirs, its success or failure is not so largely contingent upon the manner in which Claudius is portrayed; and the play probably would have succeeded even if less effective work had been done in characterizing Claudius. The fact that his character is so well drawn contributes to the sum total of what is regarded by many as Shakespeare's supreme dramatic creation.

VI. SUMMARY AND CONCLUSION

My treatment of eleven villains has been representative rather than definitive. Villains were selected from comedies, histories, and tragedies. Some of the villains dominate their plays; others have lesser roles. Most of them succeed in bringing about a catastrophe, but the villainy of two characters (Angelo and Shylock) is thwarted. Some of the villains play a lone hand, while others work in conjunction with partners. My rogues' gallery includes characters whose major crimes were committed before the play begins and those with an unblemished record prior to the opening of the play. The works in which these eleven villains appear range in time from Shakespeare's early plays (both *Titus Andronicus* and *Richard III* were written about 1592) to the period of the great tragedies, 1600-1606.

On the subject of characterization I have examined the views of some earlier critics, particularly eighteenth and nineteenth century writers, and have compared their opinions with those of twentieth century scholars. It should be apparent to the reader that I am not in complete accord with either group. Instead, I have tried to show that in the most effective plays a proper balance is maintained between character and action. The plays should not be viewed primarily as character sketches in which action is unimportant, nor should the characters be unconvincing to a present-day audience. In evaluating the effectiveness of villains, it seems to me that the fairest way is to consider the impression they make on an audience viewing the play. Inconsistencies that come to light only after close scrutiny of the printed text should not be regarded as serious flaws in character construction.

Certain conclusions emerge. First, the enthusiasm expressed by some eighteenth century and many nineteenth century critics over Shakespeare's powers of characterization tends to be sweeping and uncritical. The praise was probably justified when applied to Shakespeare's most effectively conceived villains, though obviously not when applied to a villain like Aaron, and probably not when applied to characters like Angelo, Edmund, Goneril, and Regan. Also, preoccupation with Shakespeare's characters by many critics writing before the present century made them overlook the requirements of the drama as a whole and resulted in their neglecting to define those qualities that make for effective characterization. I have emphasized such qualities as motivation, complexity, and liveliness. I have considered whether a character develops during the course of a play, and whether his actions appear to be free from obvious subservience to the demands of the plot. With reference to this latter quality the difference between Lady Macbeth and Iago should be recalled. I have shown that Iago seems to construct his own plot so that the balance between plot and character does not present a problem in his play. On the other hand, Lady Macbeth is so obviously designed to serve as a foil to her husband that Shakespeare had to sacrifice some plausibility and complexity, especially in the early scenes. I noted another example of character subserving plot in the conduct of Edmund. Though very little in his behavior during most of the play suggests that he has any spark of human kindness, he suddenly repents at the end because the plot requires it. He must tell the others about his "writ" upon the lives of Cordelia and Lear.

On the question of motivation, which I regard as one of the most important attributes of a convincing villain, I have tried to show how careful Shakespeare usually was in providing a clearly stated motive early in the play. When he neglected to do this, as with Aaron, the villain is unconvincing. I also tried to show that a convincing motive or other plausible behavior early in the play sets a tone of verisimilitude that minor inconsistencies later in the play do little to disrupt so far as the spectator is concerned. The opening scene in *Othello,* where Iago explains the reason for his animosity toward the Moor and Cassio, is a good illustration. Conversely, the incredible scene early in *Richard III,* where Richard woos Lady Anne while she is on her way to the funeral of King Henry VI, sets a tone of implausibility that may remain with the audience throughout the play.

Even more significant than the tendency of earlier critics to be all-inclusive rather than selective in praising Shakespeare's characters was their apparent unawareness of a point beyond which psychological accuracy of portrayal may detract from, rather than enhance, the effectiveness of the play. There is some evidence that Macbeth and Shylock claim so large a share of the audience's interest and sympathy that the total effect of their plays may be distorted.

In attempting to correct the bias of earlier critics, some twentieth-century scholars have gone to another extreme. If one were to believe them, he would conclude that Shakespeare, far from trying to create lifelike characters, wrote in strict accord with the conventions of the Elizabethan stage. According to these conventions, Elizabethan audiences accepted villains even without motivation and saw them as types: black, illegitimate, deformed. From these types all manner of villainy was accepted without explanation. We are told, for example, that Elizabethan audiences wasted no sympathy on villains, some of whom were unnaturally objective about their criminal nature.

Understanding these conventions helps the Shakespearean scholar; but I have attempted to show that an appeal to the conventions to account for lack of subtle characterization provides, in general, too pat an explanation. There is no conclusive evidence, for example, that audiences in the Elizabethan Age, or in any other period, were incapable either of sympathizing with the plight of Shylock, or of regarding Angelo's repentance as sincere. As for the unnatural objectivity of characters like Iago who admit their villainy and even praise the heroes, I have shown that such a convention is not peculiar to the Elizabethans, but is frequently necessary as exposition; moreover, it does not detract from a villain's effectiveness unless one takes the hypercritical viewpoint of a scholar searching for flaws, inconsistencies, and implausibilities.

Although research that uncovers the conventions of the stage is an interesting and important part of historical scholarship, playgoers of this or any other age are not likely to accept what does not seem convincing in a play merely because they are told —on however great authority—that it was all part of the convention of the day. What gives Shakespeare's best plays their universal appeal is their power to transcend limitations of time. And where this appeal is lacking, the plays have not achieved or maintained popularity; in fact they might scarcely have survived except for the eminent name of their author. I have pointed out that, even though Shakespeare wrote with the interests of Elizabethan audiences in mind, and even though he was undoubtedly aware of certain conventions of the theatre in which he worked, there is little evidence to make one believe that all his characters were formed to fit the prevailing pattern. We know that he ignored classical conventions and violated the unities; we also know that in some of his earlier plays, notably *Titus Andronicus,* where he followed the convention of using a type villain with little motivation, individuality, or complexity, he achieved a temporary, but not a lasting success.

As for the relative merits of the eleven villains considered, it is easy to say who is the least effectively characterized. In my opinion, Aaron is the only villain who is little more than a type. He lacks motivation, variety, and remorse. He acts chiefly to further the plot; and he is certainly no example of that "one supreme creator" of character whom Swinburne, and other critics before him, extolled. To go to the other extreme and decide who is the most effectively characterized villain is not so easy. I would vote for Iago. He is made credible by his intellect, his motivation, and his liveliness; and, most of all, by the fact that the plot seems to be the creation of his active brain. Claudius is another convincing villain. Though he is not nearly so lively and intellectual as Iago, and though he does not dominate his play to the extent that Iago does, he is effective chiefly because of his hypocrisy and also because his motivation is convincing and because he is given some trace of conscience. Add to these qualities the fact that villainy is only a part of his life, and we have a character who seems like a human being, even though an unsavory one.

Although some critics disagree, I regard Iago and Claudius as villains without serious flaws in characterization. They do not claim the sympathy that Macbeth and Shylock do, but their actions and the motives underlying them are understandable.

And it is perhaps better that an audience understand rather than sympathize with villains because of the point mentioned above that sympathy for a villain may detract from the effectiveness of the play. For those who insist upon sympathetic presentation of characters, even of villains, I believe that Macbeth is clearly the most sympathetically conceived of the criminals we have considered. Though we have seen that he struggles very little against being drawn into crime, the struggle is there to an extent not evident in the other villains; and this struggle makes him seem human. The steps in his disintegration are presented with verisimilitude, and the fall of so promising a man cannot help but impress the audience.

As for the other villains—Richard III, Lady Macbeth, Angelo. Shylock, Regan, Goneril, and Edmund—all of them have some motivation and some of them have other lifelike qualities; but they all seem to me to have flaws that would be noticed even by audiences not made up of Shakespearean scholars. Richard III, though in some ways one of the more effective of Shakespeare's villains, is melodramatic and, in some scenes, unconvincing; Lady Macbeth so patently subserves her husband and the demands of the plot that she does not emerge as a fully developed character in her own right; Angelo and Shylock, though both interesting villains, are characterized with such ambivalence as to obscure their author's intent; and Regan, Goneril, and Edmund, though to some extent plausible, indulge in so much physical cruelty against relatively helpless antagonists that, although no one would deny that their counterparts exist in real life, as artistic creations they seem repulsive and baffle the understanding.

NOTES

Notes on Preface to Shakespeare's Villains, pp. 11-12

1. D. C. Allen, Review of *Shakespeare Survey 4, MLN,* LXVIII, 2, Feb., 1953, p. 144.

2. L. C. Knights, *How Many Children Had Lady Macbeth?,* Cambridge, 1933, p. 1.

3. T. S. Eliot, *Shakespeare and the Stoicism of Seneca,* 1927. See *Shakespeare Criticism, 1919-35,* ed. Anne Bradby, London, 1936, p. 209.

4. H. B. Charlton, *Shakespearian Tragedy,* Cambridge, 1948, pp. vii-viii.

Notes on Introduction, pp. 15-24

1. Samuel Johnson, *Preface to Shakespeare,* 1765. See *Shakespeare Criticism,* intro. by D. Nichol Smith, London, 1916, p. 90.

2. Robert W. Babcock, *The Genesis of Shakespeare Idolatry, 1766-1799,* Chapel Hill, N. C., 1931, p. 3.

3. Dedication to *Shakespeare Illustrated,* ed. Mrs. Charlotte Ramsay Lennox, 2 vols., London, 1753. In *Samuel Johnson on Shakespeare,* ed. W. K. Wimsatt, Jr., N. Y., 1960, p. 14.

4. Alexander Pope, *Preface to Shakespeare's Works,* 1725. See D. N. Smith, *op. cit.,* p. 48.

5. D. N. Smith, *op. cit.,* p. xvi.

6. Maurice Morgann, *An Essay on the Dramatic Character of Sir John Falstaff,* 1777. See D. N. Smith, *op. cit.,* p. 194.

7. S. T. Coleridge, *Lectures,* 1818. See D. N. Smith, *op. cit.,* p. 258.

8. William Hazlitt, *Characters of Shakespeare's Plays,* 1817. See *The Collected Works of William Hazlitt,* 13 vols., ed. A. R. Waller and Arnold Glover, London, 1902. I:74.

9. A. C. Swinburne, *General Introduction to the Works of Shakespeare.* See *The Comedies of Shakespeare,* ed. W. J. Craig, (Oxford Edition) London, 1932, p. v.

10. Logan P. Smith, *On Reading Shakespeare,* New York, 1933, pp. 152-153.

11. Charles Lamb, *On the Tragedies of Shakespeare, considered with reference to their fitness for Stage Representation,* 1811. See D. N. Smith, *op. cit.,* pp. 219, 220, 222, 232.

12. Elmer Edgar Stoll, *Shakespeare Studies,* revised edition, New York, 1942, p. 259.

13. *Ibid,* p. 257.

14. George P. Baker, *The Development of Shakespeare as a Dramatist,* New York, 1907, pp. 263-264.

15. Muriel C. Bradbrook, *Themes and Conventions of Elizabethan Tragedy,* London, 1935, pp. 50-51.

16. *Ibid,* p. 65.

17. *Heine on Shakespeare,* ed. Ida Benecke, Westminster, 1895, pp. 125-126.

18. Stoll, *op. cit.,* p. 393.

19. John I. M. Stewart, *Character and Motive in Shakespeare,* London, 1949, p. 46.

20. Bradbrook, *op. cit.,* p. 40. According to Dr. Edgar, Allardyce Nicoll (see *Studies in Shakespeare,* N. Y., 1928), was another critic who solved "the problem [the absurdity of Lear's dividing his kingdom as he did] by explaining away all the improbabilities and absurdities in *King Lear* on the grounds that Shakespeare only followed an older play, *King Leir.* Indeed, this older play, which was undoubtedly Shakespeare's immediate source, does give acceptable motivation for Lear's actions; for here, King Leir, after the death of his queen, feeling unable in the task of governing his three daughters, for 'fathers best do govern sons,' decides to divide the kingdom among the three of them. Goneril and Regan have been provided with husbands. But Cordella objects to any husband chosen for her 'unless love allows.' Leir, therefore, decides to ask for public professions of his daughters' loves in order to trap Cordella into some extravagant verbal expression of her love for him, upon which he is merely to ask her such a simple request as marrying a King of Brittany, 'which she cannot well deny. . . .' This, of course, is definite motivation for the trial of professions, entirely lacking in Shakespeare's *King Lear.*" Irving I. Edgar, M.D., "Shakespeare's Psychopathological Knowledge: a Study in Criticism and Interpretation," *Journal of Abnormal and Social Psychology,* Vol. XXX, No. 1, April-June, 1935, p. 81.

21. G. Wilson Knight, *The Shakespearian Tempest,* London, 1932, p. 7.

22. Mary Lascelles, *Shakespeare's Measure for Measure,* London, 1953, p. 89.

23. Bradbrook, *op. cit.,* p. 58.

24. John P. Cutts, Review of C. N. Coe, *Shakespeare's Villains.* In *Shakespeare Quarterly,* IX, 3, 1958, p. 417.

Notes on Chapter II, Aaron and Iago, pp. 25-46

1. *The Tragedy of Titus Andronicus,* ed. A. M. Witherspoon, *The Yale Shakespeare,* New Haven, 1926, p. 116.

2. *Palladis Tamia* . . . by Francis Meres, London, 1598. In J. Q. Adams, *A Life of William Shakespeare,* Boston, 1923, p. 238.

3. *The Complete Works of Shakespeare,* ed. G. L. Kittredge, Boston, 1936, p. 971.

4. Quotations from Shakespeare's plays are from Kittredge, *op. cit.*

5. Ruth L. Anderson, *Elizabethan Psychology and Shakespeare's Plays,* University of Iowa, Humanistic Studies, 1927, III:4, p. 144.

6. G. B. Harrison, *Shakespeare's Tragedies,* London, 1951, pp. 31-32.

7. Ralph M. Sargent, "The Source of *Titus Andronicus,*" *Studies in Philology,* XLVI, 2, April, 1949, pp. 176-177.

8. Clifford Leech, "The Year's Contribution to Shakespearian Study," *Shakespeare Survey,* No. 12, 1959, pp. 135-136.

9. Stoll, *Shakespeare Studies,* p. 382.

10. Bradbrook, *op. cit.,* p. 63.

11. A. C. Bradley, *Shakespearean Tragedy,* 2nd ed., London, 1937, pp. 211-213.

12. Robert B. Heilman, *Magic in the Web,* Lexington, Kentucky, 1956, pp. 25-26.

13. *Ibid.,* p. 26.

14. *Ibid.,* p. 29.

15. *Ibid.,* p. 29.

16. *Ibid.,* p. 41.

17. *Ibid.,* p. 40.

18. *Ibid.,* p. 13.

19. Cinthio's Novels, No. 7. In *Othello, A New Variorum Edition,* ed. Furness, 7th ed., 1886, pp. 378-379.

20. *Coleridge's Shakespearean Criticism,* ed. Thomas M. Raysor, 2 vols., Cambridge, Mass., 1930, 1:49.

21. Heilman, *op. cit.*, p. 33.

22. E. E. Stoll, *Art and Artifice in Shakespeare*, London, 1933, p. 7.

23. August Goll, *Criminal Types in Shakespeare*, translated by Mrs. Charles Weekes, London, 1909, p. 213.

24. *Ibid.*, pp. 216-217.

25. *Ibid.*, pp. 217-218.

26. Stoll, *Art and Artifice in Shakespeare*, p. 10.

Notes on Chapter III, Richard III, Macbeth, and Lady Macbeth, pp. 47-68

1. Charles L. Kingsford, "Richard III," *Encyclopaedia Britannica*, 1956, 19:288.

2. Bernard Spivack, *Shakespeare and the Allegory of Evil*, New York, 1958, pp. 387-388.

3. Anderson, *op. cit.*, p. 144.

4. Stoll, *Shakespeare Studies*, p. 346.

5. *Ibid.*, pp. 347-348.

6. Henry Reed, *Lectures on English History and Tragic Poetry as Illustrated by Shakspeare*, Philadelphia, 1856, p. 324.

7. Edward Dowden, "Introduction to *Richard III.*" In *The Histories and Poems of Shakespeare*, Oxford Edition, London, 1932, p. 735.

8. George Steevens, In *A New Variorum Edition of Shakespeare, the Tragedy of Richard the Third* . . . , 2nd. ed., ed. Horace H. Furness, Jr., Philadelphia, 1909, p. 573.

9. *Ibid.*, pp. 549-572.

10. Thomas Whately, *Remarks on Some of the Characters of Shakespeare*, 3rd. ed., London, 1839, pp. 27-28.

11. Spivack, *op. cit.*, p. 37.

12. Anna B. Jameson, *Shakespeare's Female Characters*, 2nd. ed., Bielefeld, 1843, pp. 338-340.

13. *Ibid.*, p. 341.

14. See *The Shakespeare Papers of the Late William Maginn*, annotated by Dr. Shelton Mackenzie, Redfield, N.Y., 1856, p. 186.

15. *Coleridge's Shakespearean Criticism*, ed. Raysor, II:271.

16. Bradley, *op. cit.*, pp. 484-486.

17. *Coleridge's Shakespearean Criticism*, ed. Raysor, II:217.

18. *The Complete Works of Shakespeare*, ed. Kittredge, pp. 1113, 788.

19. E. K. Chambers, *William Shakespeare,* 2 vols., Oxford, 1930, I:303.

20. Bradley, *op. cit.,* p. 359.

21. *Ibid.,* p. 344.

22. For various theories on this subject, see Bradley, *op. cit.,* pp. 480-484.

23. Clarence V. Boyer, *The Villain as Hero in Elizabethan Tragedy,* London, 1914, p. 189.

24. Margaret Webster, *Shakespeare Today,* London, 1957, pp. 223-224.

25. *The Shakespeare Papers of the Late William Maginn,* pp. 169-170.

Notes on Chapter IV, Angelo and Shylock, pp. 69-87

1. Bradbrook, *op. cit.,* p. 60.

2. *Coleridge's Shakespearean Criticism,* ed. Raysor, I:113-114.

3. A. C. Swinburne, *A Study of Shakespeare,* London, 1880, pp. 151-153.

4. W.M.T. Dodds, "The Character of Angelo in *Measure for Measure,*" *MLR,* XLI, 1946, pp. 246-247.

5. Kenneth Muir, *Shakespeare's Sources I, Comedies and Tragedies,* London, 1957, p. 102.

6. Stewart, *op. cit.,* p. 141, n. 30.

7. Herman Sinsheimer, *Shylock; the History of a Character or the Myth of the Jew,* with a foreword by John Middleton Murry, London, 1947, p. 10.

8. *The Merchant of Venice, The New Hudson Shakespeare,* introduction and notes by Henry N. Hudson, Boston, 1879, p. xxvi.

9. Murry, *op. cit.,* p. 12.

10. Stoll, *Shakespeare Studies,* p. 272.

11. John Palmer, *Comic Characters of Shakespeare,* London, 1946, p. 55.

12. *Ibid.,* pp. 58-59.

13. L. B. Wright and V. L. Freund, eds., *The Merchant of Venice, The Folger Library General Reader's Shakespeare,* N.Y., 1957, p. ix.

14. Palmer, *op. cit.,* p. 56.

15. Edward Dowden, "Introduction to *The Merchant of Venice,*" *The Comedies of Shakespeare,* p. 589.

16. H. B. Charlton, "Shakespeare's Jew," *Bulletin of the John*

Rylands Library, Manchester University Press, Vol. 18, 1934, pp. 34-68.

17. Palmer, *op. cit.,* p. 88.

Notes on Chapter V, Regan, Goneril, Edmund, and Claudius, pp. 88-106

1. See *supra,* p. 17.
2. *Coleridge's Shakespearean Criticism,* ed. Raysor, I:55.
3. Agnes M. Mackenzie, *The Women in Shakespeare's Plays,* London 1942, p. 295.
4. *Ibid.,* pp. 294-295.
5. *Ibid.,* p. 314.
6. *Ibid.,* pp. 313-314.
7. *Ibid.,* p. 310.
8. *Coleridge's Shakespearean Criticism,* ed. Raysor, I:56-57.
9. *The Tragedy of King Lear,* ed. Kittredge, Boston, 1940, p. 119.
10. Bertram Joseph, *Conscience and the King: a Study of Hamlet,* London, 1953, pp. 53-54.
11. Levin L. Schücking, *Character Problems in Shakespeare's Plays,* N.Y., 1922, p. 172.
12. *Ibid.,* p. 176.
13. Anderson, *op. cit.,* pp. 152-153.
14. Bernard Grebanier, *The Heart of Hamlet,* N.Y., 1960, pp. 268-269.
15. Howard M. Jones, "The King in Hamlet," *University of Texas Bulletin* No. 1865, Nov. 20, 1918, pp. 89-90, 29-30, 32, 43.

INDEX